Happy Birthday
1985!
Love,
Joan + John

Fresh Garden Vegetables

LIBBY HILLMAN

ILLUSTRATED BY JOAN BLUME

HARPER & ROW, PUBLISHERS, New York

Cambridge, Philadelphia, San Francisco, London

Mexico City, São Paulo, Sydney

IRENA CHALMERS COOKBOOKS, INC., New York

FIRST HARPER & ROW EDITION 1983

Library of Congress Cataloging in Publication Data
Hillman, Libby.
　Fresh garden vegetables.
　(Great American cooking schools)
　1. Cookery (Vegetables)　I. Title.　II. Series:
Great American cooking schools (Harper & Row)
TX801.H55 1983　　641.6′5　　82-48667
ISBN 0-06-015157-9

83 84 85 86 87 10 9 8 7 6 5 4 3 2 1

Contents

Introduction

Vegetables are a joy. There is the esthetic pleasure of their many colors and textures. A carrot may be crisp and crunchy, perfect for a garnish or salad, or cooked until soft and then pureed; a potato can have as many personalities as you care to give it. Vegetables vary enormously in flavor and afford the imaginative cook endless versatility. They can make a simple meal festive and have the double merit of being low in calories and high in nutritional value.

As Americans have traveled more and more in the past 20 years, they have developed a taste for the lesser-known or more exotic vegetables they have encountered abroad. The resulting demand has slowly had an effect on the large commercial growers and ultimately on the supermarkets, so that many "new" vegetables are now available for both the beginner and the experienced cook to discover and enjoy. In addition, certain cooking techniques borrowed from other lands, such as Chinese stir-frying, have become popular.

Thanks to improved transportation and refrigeration methods as well as advances in agricultural science, it is now possible to buy formerly seasonal vegetables almost year round. Strawberries in winter are certainly a treat, but I believe that some foods are worth waiting for. I would rather anticipate the succulent Northeastern sweet corn which ripens in July and August, for instance, than the transported winter varieties of the South or, worse yet, the frozen and packaged versions. I'll pass up winter tomatoes and wait for the local vine-ripened ones. It is a nice luxury to have one's own garden or a farm stand nearby, but it is possible even for city-dwellers to grow some of their own vegetables in window boxes or on a terrace and the rewards are definitely worth the effort.

Select vegetables carefully, inspecting each piece (gently!) when you are allowed to choose them yourself. Pick a reliable vegetable shop or supermarket by judging the care it takes with its produce and observing the frequency of its deliveries. Root vegetables may be stored in any cool corner or closet (50 to 60 degrees); store all other vegetables in the refrigerator. Some leafy vegetables should be wrapped in toweling or in special plastic boxes to keep them crisp. Parsley and watercress should be washed before being put away; otherwise, do not wash vegetables before storing them.

Cooking vegetables *al dente*, so that they are still firm, preserves vitamins and gives the vegetables better texture and flavor. When a recipe calls for boiling a vegetable in salted water the ratio is generally ½ teaspoon salt to 2 quarts water; if more salt or other seasonings are needed, I prefer to add them after boiling. Steaming, stir-frying, sautéing and broiling, as well as other techniques, are all discussed and used in the recipes that follow, along with variations and suggestions for leftovers. I always save the liquid in which vegetables have been cooked for use as a base for the sauce or for soups and stews.

A fond memory from my childhood is that of our Thursday dinners, which were entirely vegetarian. In addition to saving money, my mother was preparing our digestive tracts with a light, meatless meal before the weekend repasts. Obviously, my addiction to vegetables began at an early age. I am still constantly surprised and challenged by the endless possibilities of vegetable cooking, and look forward to sharing my old and new favorites with you.

About the Ingredients

BUTTER: Always buy unsalted butter. Store it in the freezer and defrost it as you need it.

Many cooks like to use clarified butter for sautéing because it can be heated to a high temperature without danger of burning. The nonfat parts of the fresh butter, the casein and whey, cause the butter to burn rapidly, leaving black specks on the food being cooked. Clarified butter can be prepared ahead and refrigerated for several weeks. The addition of oil to fresh butter will also prevent the butter from burning when it is used for frying vegetables.

Clarified Butter: Clarify a large quantity—at least 1 or 2 pounds—of unsalted butter at a time to justify the effort. Melt the butter over medium heat, taking care not to let it brown. Skim the white froth from the surface. Save the clear yellow center part, the clarified butter, and refrigerate the white residue (whey) remaining at the bottom. There will still be butterfat in this mixture, which will rise to the top and solidify as it cools. Add this to the other clarified butter and discard the remaining whey.

BOUQUET GARNI: The traditional bouquet is used frequently in sauces, soups and stews. It consists of a dozen black peppercorns, a few sprigs of fresh parsley, thyme and a bay leaf. These are tied together with string in a piece of cheesecloth, simmered with other ingredients, and discarded later. When fresh thyme or parsley is not available, use half a teaspoon of the dried herb instead; add it directly into the pot.

LEMONS AND ORANGES: Always use these fruits and their juices and rinds fresh.

PARMESAN AND GRUYÈRE CHEESE: Buy a wedge (at least 1 pound) and grate or slice it as you need it. If grated cheese is left over, freeze it for the next time.

PARSLEY, CHIVES AND DILL: Always use fresh when available.

All Other Herbs: The amounts given are for dried herbs. Use fresh ones if you can; they are more fragrant and more flavorful. Fresh herbs are used in three times the quantity compared with their dried counterparts. Be careful with strong herbs such as sage and rosemary, trusting your nose and palate to guide you. Be adventurous in substituting and adding herbs.

SALT: I like to use kosher salt for cooking. You should try a salt tasting one day; there are many kinds of salt available, and they all have different characteristics.

If you are on a salt-free diet, substitute pepper, herbs, spices, vinegar and lemon juice and after a while you will hardly miss the salt.

PEPPER: Always use freshly ground pepper, white for light sauces and black for almost everything else.

SPICES: If spices are available in seed or bean form, grind them yourself. There are many small grinders on the market.

VEGETABLE BROTH: Refrigerate or freeze the cooking liquid from vegetables for use in soups, stews, and sauces. Discard the liquid from strong-tasting vegetables unless you have a specific use for it.

Recipes

In the following recipes, this * signifies the point to
which a dish can be prepared ahead of time.

Artichokes

The artichoke is one of nature's greatest accomplishments. A relative of the ordinary thistle, it is a puzzling vegetable to the uninitiated—and an object of passionate devotion for food lovers everywhere. It thrives in unimaginable abundance about 100 miles south of San Francisco around the town of Castroville. There is a small restaurant there—a truck drivers' stop—that offers on its menu 30 or 40 different ways to eat artichokes.

When cooked, the artichoke becomes two vegetables, One is the leafy outer part; the other is the meaty white base. The base (*fond d'artichaut*) and the heart (*coeur d'artichaut*) are terms that are used interchangeably, yet they are not exactly the same. The bottom, the *fond*, is stripped of all the leaves, then shaped smoothly with a small sharp knife and cleaned of every morsel of fuzz (choke) and greenery. My new students are always surprised when they first see the leaves snapped away to leave the small, cuplike base. The heart, on the other hand, is served with the smallest and most tender inner leaves. The heart of the artichoke can be quartered, sliced, fried or braised. All these are methods characteristic of French and Italian cooking. Young, tender artichokes can be cooked and eaten, choke and all.

The leafy whole artichoke is a challenge for all good cooks. It can be boiled, steamed, braised or fried, and served hot or cold. It is interesting to see how profoundly the artichoke affects the taste buds, and changes the way other flavors are perceived. It is for this reason that artichokes are best eaten as a separate course; I wouldn't serve them with a very subtly seasoned entree or a delicate wine.

Cleaning and Preparing

Cut the stem flat to permit the artichoke to stand upright without tipping. Cut off about one inch across the top leaves and rub the top and bottom with half a lemon. Break off the tough outer leaves and trim around the bottom with a paring knife where the leaves were snapped off. Trim the tips of the other leaves with scissors. When artichoke leaves are trimmed and exposed to the air, the tips discolor quickly. Be sure to keep a stainless steel or glass bowl handy. Fill it with cold water to which a little lemon juice has been added. Dip the artichokes into this acidulated water.

When boiling artichokes, add a tablespoon of lemon juice or vinegar and at least one teaspoon of salt to every quart of water. Be sure to use a non-aluminum saucepan or casserole or the artichokes will develop an odd taste. Choose a pot that will accommodate the artichokes snugly side by side; otherwise, they will float to the surface of the water. If you must use too large a pot, weight the artichokes with a heatproof plate to keep them under water.

Boiled Artichokes (Hot or Cold)

4-6 medium-size artichokes
2-3 tablespoons fresh lemon juice
2-3 teaspoons salt
1 medium-size onion, sliced
  (optional)
1 bay leaf (optional)
1 clove garlic, peeled (optional)

Wash and trim the artichokes as described in the introduction.

Fill a saucepan with enough salted water to cover the artichokes. Add the lemon juice and salt and bring to a boil, adding the optional ingredients if desired. Drop the artichokes into the boiling water, weighting them down if they float. Cook, uncovered, for 30 to 40 minutes, depending on size.

Test them for doneness by pulling off a bottom leaf; it should come away easily. Also pierce the bottom of the heart with a fork to check softness. Remove the artichokes from the water with tongs or a slotted spoon, turn them upside down on a plate, and squeeze them gently to drain off the water.

To serve the artichokes, gently open the center and twist out the cone of soft leaves; use a spoon to scrape off the fuzz on the bottom of the vegetable, trying not to dent the bottom. Turn the cone of leaves upside down on top of the artichoke so that it will resemble an opened flower. Serve hot or cold.

HOT: Place a small bowl of clarified butter or Hollandaise Sauce (see page 82) on the side of each plate for dipping, or spoon the hollandaise into the center cavity.

COLD: Give each person a small serving bowl of vinaigrette sauce, hollandaise, or mustard mayonnaise on the side for dipping. Alternatively, set the artichoke in the center of a round plate, remove the leaves and arrange them in a circular pattern; scrape out the choke and cut the bottom into segments. Serve with one of the cold sauces mentioned above.

Fried Artichoke Hearts

Fried artichokes are delicious. You can use frozen artichoke hearts or the canned variety from Spain, but these cannot compare with the fresh vegetable.

6-8 medium-size artichokes
Juice of 2 lemons
4 teaspoons salt
½ cup flour
¼ teaspoon pepper
1 cup breadcrumbs
2 eggs
2 tablespoons water
2 to 3 cups oil (mixture of vegetable and olive)
¼ cup finely chopped Italian parsley

Wash and trim the artichokes and soak them in a bowl of cold water. Add the juice of 1 lemon to the water.

Starting from the base, bend the leaves out and snip them off close to the bottom. Work around toward the top as you come to the light-colored center. Cut across the artichoke about 1½ inches from the bottom. Remove any prickly purple leaves and trim around the bottom for a smooth surface.

If the stem is long, cut off the end. Peel the dark green outer layer, keeping the stem attached. Rub all exposed areas with lemon as you work. Cut each artichoke lengthwise into 6 parts.

Boil at least 3 quarts of water with the juice of the remaining lemon and 1 tablespoon salt. Add the artichokes and cook them for 5 to 7 minutes. Drain and dry them well. Remove the choke by scraping gently from the bottom.*

Spread 2 sheets of wax paper on a counter. Sprinkle the flour, ½ teaspoon salt and pepper on one, and breadcrumbs on the other. Beat the eggs with ½ teaspoon salt and 2 tablespoons of water.

Heat the oil in a deep-fat fryer or deep skillet to 325 degrees. Meanwhile, dip the artichoke hearts first in the flour mixture, then in the beaten egg mixture, and finally in the breadcrumbs.*

Fry the pieces for 3 minutes and drain them on paper towels spread over wire cake-cooling racks. To make sure the hearts fry evenly, take care not to crowd the fryer.*

Increase the temperature of the oil to 375 degrees and fry the hearts again for 2 or 3 minutes just before serving, to crisp them. Drain on the paper towels and serve, sprinkled with parsley, on a napkin or doily.

NOTE: Advance preparation can be divided into 3 parts as designated by asterisks. Once the artichokes have been boiled, they will keep in the refrigerator for 4 or 5 days covered with the water in which they were cooked. Add a teaspoon of oil to the water. Breading and coating can be done several hours or as much as a day before the final frying.

Serve fried artichokes with rice or pasta, or as one of the vegetables in *fritto misto*.

Stuffed Artichokes

Twenty years ago I stopped for lunch in the Italian village of Acquapendente. The antipasto tray included a stuffed artichoke, which inspired this recipe.

4 artichokes
½ lemon
2 tablespoons lemon juice
4 tablespoons olive oil
1 teaspoon finely chopped garlic
¼ cup Parmesan cheese
2 anchovies, mashed
¼ cup freshly made coarse
    breadcrumbs
2 tablespoons finely chopped parsley
½ teaspoon oregano
½ teaspoon salt
½ teaspoon pepper
1 cup chicken broth

Wash and trim each artichoke as suggested in the introduction. Spread the leaves and twist out the cone of leaves in the center. Using a teaspoon or a melon-ball cutter, reach into the bottom and carefully scoop out the choke until the bottom is white and clean, then rub the inside with a slice of lemon. Drop the cleaned artichokes into a bowl of cold water with lemon juice.

To prepare the stuffing, mix 2 tablespoons oil with all the other ingredients except the broth. Divide into 4 portions.

Drain the artichokes well. Fill the center and spaces between the leaves with the stuffing. Place the artichokes in a saucepan with the broth. Drizzle the remaining 2 tablespoons of oil over the artichokes, cover, and simmer for 30 to 40 minutes.

This is an excellent luncheon dish served with crusty bread and thinly sliced Italian salami. The artichokes are best eaten at room temperature.

An interesting variation is to stuff the artichokes with your favorite meat-loaf recipe. Cook the same way as above or bake in a covered casserole at 350 degrees for 1 hour.

Arugula

The Italians popularized this unusual salad green, now offered frequently in both restaurants and markets. (It is sometimes called rocket, or in French, *rockette*.) Although arugula is brought to market with roots and tender leaves intact because it wilts and perishes so fast, it is nevertheless a hardy plant in the garden, and continues to grow after it is cut. I enjoy the mature leaves and flowers as well as the tender young ones. In a salad, arugula is best served alone with a vinaigrette dressing. Cousin to the mustard family, it resembles the radish leaf and has some of its bitterness along with its own distinctively nutty flavor.

Fettucini and Arugula   *Serves 4*

Although I generally prefer arugula alone or with watercress and Boston lettuce in a cold salad, I have at times combined it with freshly cooked pasta for a change of texture and taste.

1 bunch arugula (½ pound)
½ pound fettucini
½ cup olive oil
1 tablespoon finely chopped garlic
**Salt and freshly ground pepper
    to taste**
¼ cup grated Parmesan cheese

Warm the plates or serving bowls in a very low oven.

Cut the arugula just above the root. Wash the leaves thoroughly in several baths of cold water. Boil the fettucini in salted water, and add the arugula to the pot 1 minute before the pasta is ready (*al dente*) so that the arugula will just be parboiled.

While the pasta is cooking, heat the olive oil in a saucepan, add the garlic and cook for 2 minutes, being careful not to let it burn. Pour the garlic and oil into a warm serving bowl.

Drain the fettucini and arugula well; immediately turn them into the bowl with the oil and garlic. Adjust the seasoning.

Toss well with Parmesan cheese, and serve immediately on the heated plates or bowls.

NOTE: Potato salad and arugula go particularly well together for a cold buffet.

Asparagus

Asparagus is the sign of spring in our Northeastern marketplace. The winter imports from south of the border do not entice me—I prefer to wait for the plump and succulent California variety, which is soon followed by the New Jersey harvest when the climate cooperates. Buy asparagus when it is freshly green, firm, smooth and closed at the tips. The young thin stalks are delicious raw or barely cooked. I love the fat, large stalks even if the bottoms are slightly woody (they can be lightly peeled at the ends).

If you watch people eating asparagus, you will know where they come from. The Europeans—who eat almost everything else with two utensils—pick up asparagus with their fingers to savor it to the very end of the stalk; in Europe, therefore, asparagus is always served peeled. Americans generally cut and eat asparagus with a fork, discarding the tough ends which have not been peeled.

Fresh asparagus tied in a bunch makes a beautiful centerpiece; it has been an inspiration for porcelain and faïence as well as cookery.

When you buy asparagus, immediately store it, unwashed, in the refrigerator. Place the stalks upright in a jar or lay them in a flat-bottomed pan with two inches of water, and cover the pan with plastic wrap. (This is also a good way to preserve parsley and arugula.)

How much asparagus to serve depends on personal appetites and on the position of the vegetables in the menu; four stalks per person for a side dish, three if the stalks are stir-fried, and eight for a first course or luncheon entree.

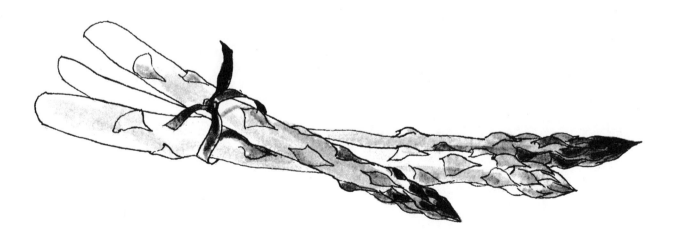

Boiled Asparagus

Wash the asparagus stalks in cold water; cut them into uniform lengths and peel the stems with a vegetable peeler. Choose a pan in which the asparagus can lie flat or a tall saucepan in which the stalks can stand upright. If you wish, tie individual portions with soft string.

If you are using a flat pan, boil enough salted water to cover the asparagus. When the water boils, place the asparagus in the pan and cook 4 to 5 minutes. Always cook an extra spear for testing if you are unsure of the proper timing.

If you use a tall, narrow saucepan, boil enough salted water to reach 1 inch below the tips of the asparagus. When the water boils, stand the asparagus in it. Boil for 2 or 3 minutes, then cover the tips with an inverted pot or aluminum foil and boil for another 2 minutes. Incidentally, an old-fashioned coffee percolator can be substituted for a tall saucepan.

NOTE: To steam asparagus, use a rack and make sure the boiling water comes up to just below it. Place the asparagus on the rack and cover the pot. Steam for 7 to 10 minutes.

Two-Minute Asparagus

Serves 2

6 tender, young, thin asparagus
  spears
½ cup cottage cheese
2 tablespoons sour cream
½ teaspoon sweet Hungarian
  paprika
1 tablespoon finely chopped chives
  or young scallions

Wash the asparagus, cut it into 1-inch slices, and then cook it in salted boiling water for 2 minutes. Drain the asparagus. Mix the cottage cheese with the sour cream and paprika, and pour the mixture over the asparagus. Serve immediately, garnished with chives or scallions.

NOTE: As a luncheon dish, this goes well with 1 cup cooked egg noodles. If the noodles are freshly made, they can be boiled with the asparagus. If they are the packaged kind, they will require more cooking time and should be cooked separately.

Asparagus au Gratin

Serves 4

12 spears asparagus
1 cup heavy cream
¼ cup finely chopped shallots
1 fresh tomato, quartered
½ medium-size onion, finely
    chopped
1 bay leaf
1 clove
¼ cup breadcrumbs
4 ounces ham, julienned
½ teaspoon salt
¼ teaspoon pepper
Few grains cayenne
¼ cup grated Parmesan cheese

Preheat the oven to 375 degrees and butter a shallow 9-inch baking dish.

Wash the asparagus. Cut the spears diagonally into 2-inch pieces. Blanch the asparagus by plunging it into boiling water for 1 minute. Drain, and set it aside.

Mix the cream, shallots, tomato, onion, bay leaf and clove in a saucepan. Simmer for 10 minutes to reduce the cream to two-thirds of the original quantity.

Sprinkle half of the breadcrumbs over the bottom of the prepared baking dish. Spread the asparagus and ham evenly over the breadcrumbs. When the cream is reduced, strain it into a bowl, season it with the salt, pepper and cayenne. Add the Parmesan and pour it over the asparagus and ham. Sprinkle the top with the remaining breadcrumbs.*

Bake, uncovered, for 15 minutes.

NOTE: This can be prepared 1 hour to 1 day ahead and refrigerated until you are ready to bake it.

For an interesting variation, leave the asparagus in whole spears, wrap each one in ham, and proceed with the recipe.

Baked Asparagus with Cheese

Serves 6

1½ pounds asparagus
6 tablespoons breadcrumbs
½ teaspoon salt
¼ teaspoon pepper
4 tablespoons butter, melted
2 eggs, separated
¼ cup each grated cheddar and
    Gruyère cheese
¼ teaspoon nutmeg

Wash the asparagus and cut it into 3-inch lengths. Boil 3 quarts of salted water and cook the asparagus, uncovered, for 3 minutes. Drain.

Mix the breadcrumbs, ¼ teaspoon salt and ⅛ teaspoon pepper with the melted butter and spread into a 10-inch round, shallow ovenproof dish. Lay the asparagus on the bed of breadcrumbs.*

Beat the egg yolks with the cheeses. Beat the egg whites until they are stiff and then fold them into the egg-cheese mixture. Season with the nutmeg and the remaining salt and pepper. Pour this over the asparagus and bake for 15 minutes.

NOTE: Other cooked vegetables such as broccoli, green beans and cauliflower may be substituted for the asparagus.

Avocado

The avocado is actually a fruit, but it is generally served as a vegetable. Called "poor man's butter" in Mexico, avocados are more of a luxury in this country, except on the West Coast, where they grow in abundance. It is difficult to find ripe, unblemished avocados in the market when you need them, so buy them a week or so in advance and ripen them in a paper bag. Avocados should be slightly soft to the touch and are most flavorful when they can be spread like butter.

Use a stainless-steel knife to spread avocado and be sure to rub the cut surfaces of the fruit with lemon to prevent discoloration. For the same reason, keep the pit in the cavity if you are storing a cut section. A cut avocado can be refrigerated for several days without spoiling.

Avocado au Gratin
Serves 4

2 tablespoons butter
2 tablespoons finely chopped
   shallots
1 teaspoon finely chopped garlic
¼ cup diced green pepper
¼ cup diced red pepper
½ cup tomato, skinned, seeded and
   diced
2 tablespoons flour
1½ cups warm milk, chicken broth,
   or combination
2 tablespoons lemon juice
1 teaspoon Worcestershire sauce
⅛ teaspoon cayenne
1 teaspoon salt
½ teaspoon pepper
2 avocados, peeled

Heat the butter in a saucepan. Add the shallots and the garlic, and fry for 2 minutes until they are glazed. Add the green and red pepper and tomato and stir gently for 1 or 2 minutes. Stir in the flour and cook it gently for another 1 or 2 minutes. Pour in the liquid and stir the mixture until it is smooth. Add the seasonings. Simmer for 5 minutes, then set aside.

Cut the avocados in half lengthwise. (Twist the halves with both hands and they will come apart.) Discard the pits. Place the avocado halves in a baking dish, pour in ½ inch of hot water and bake for 10 minutes.

Reheat the sauce. Drain the avocados and fill their cavities with the sauce. Serve at once. If there is any leftover sauce, serve it on the side.

NOTE: For a luncheon or light supper entree, add cooked seafood, fish or chicken to the sauce.

Bean Sprouts

Stir-Fried Bean Sprouts

Serves 4

Many people have had fun sprouting mung beans, the most commonly used bean sprouts. There is no need to use canned sprouts because fresh ones are now sold in almost all supermarkets. Keep them refrigerated in water, changing the water every other day. Bean sprouts alone, or with other greens, make wonderful salads. Stir-fried, they make a good side dish with any simple broiled fish or meat, or as part of a Chinese meal.

2 tablespoons vegetable or
    peanut oil
2 cloves garlic, finely chopped
1 onion, finely chopped
1 pound bean sprouts
¼ cup chicken broth
1 tablespoon sherry
1 teaspoon soy sauce
½ teaspoon sugar
¼ teaspoon pepper
1 tablespoon cornstarch mixed with
    2 tablespoons water (optional)

Heat the oil until it is very hot. Add the garlic and allow it to brown; then discard it. Add the onion and stir with a spoon in each hand for rapid and even cooking. Add the bean sprouts and stir-fry for 2 minutes. Add all the remaining ingredients and stir-fry until the liquid thickens slightly. Taste and adjust the seasoning.

Beans

Easily grown, stored and cooked, beans have been one of the most important of all foods for thousands of years. They are an important source of protein, vitamins, minerals and carbohydrates in parts of the world where animal protein is scarce.

    For cooking purposes, there are two categories of beans: those that are eaten fresh, such as green beans, and those that are eaten dried, such as limas and kidney beans.

Green beans were once called string beans, and many people still use that term, to the chagrin of the growers, who developed a string-free strain many decades ago. The terms yellow beans and wax beans designate the same vegetable.

Steam beans if you wish, but I prefer to boil them in plenty of water for four minutes. This method results in beans of excellent color and texture for both hot and cold dishes.

Fava Beans (Broad Beans) *Serves 4*

The broad bean has become a staple in European countries and is finally finding its way to American markets. The large green pods are shelled, and the flat beans (seeds) are then eaten fresh or dried. Sometimes fresh fava beans have tough skins and must be peeled before cooking. Not so long ago I was amused to find just three cooked and thinly sliced fava beans served with the entree at a restaurant specializing in nouvelle cuisine. Try these beans as a new accompaniment to lamb or pork.

1½ tablespoons butter
3 pounds fava beans in the pod
4 slices fresh tomato
½ teaspoon wine vinegar
1 tablespoon olive oil
1 tablespoon breadcrumbs
⅛ teaspoon each salt, pepper and allspice
1 slice cooked and finely chopped bacon (optional)
4 leaves fresh basil

Preheat the oven to 375 degrees and butter an 8- or 9-inch ovenproof dish with ½ tablespoon butter.

Shell the beans. If the skins are tough, peel them with a small knife. Cook, uncovered, in boiling salted water for 8 to 10 minutes or until they are tender. Drain.

Place the tomato slices in the buttered dish, drizzle the vinegar and oil over each slice, and bake in the preheated oven for 5 minutes. Toss the fava beans with the remaining butter, the breadcrumbs and the seasonings. Place a few beans on each slice of tomato, top with the bacon, and bake for 3 minutes. Arrange on individual dishes and garnish each tomato slice with a fresh basil leaf.

Beans and Shallots

1 pound green or yellow beans
2 tablespoons butter or oil
¼ cup finely chopped shallots
Salt and pepper

Wash the beans and snap off the tips. Bring 3 quarts of salted water to a boil.

Heat the butter or oil in a 10- or 12-inch skillet. When the foam subsides, add the shallots. Cook for a few minutes until the shallots look glazed; take care not to burn them. Set aside.*

Immerse the beans in boiling water and cover. When the water is boiling again, uncover and continue cooking for about 4 minutes. Drain well.

Add the beans to the skillet with the shallots. Turn on the heat; add the salt and pepper to taste, and cook for 2 minutes until they are hot. An extra morsel of butter will improve the flavor if you can afford the calories.

NOTE: The beans may be cut diagonally in 1- or 2-inch pieces, or they may be cut in long slivers, French style.

THREE VARIATIONS

Beans Italian-style: substitute olive oil for the butter and 1 tablespoon finely chopped garlic for the shallots.

Beans Provençal: use olive oil, garlic, ¼ cup chopped tomatoes and 1 teaspoon dried basil, and cook all these ingredients together.

Beans Chinese-style: slice the beans and stir-fry them with 1 tablespoon of oil, 2 slices of fresh ginger root and ¼ cup of chicken broth. Add 1 tablespoon of sherry and 1 teaspoon of soy sauce.

Cuban Black Beans

Serves 8-10

This recipe is a variation of my Cuban Black Bean Soup. After a number of reheatings—with some liquid lost each time—I discovered that the leftover beans were excellent when served with rice. This dish is a vegetarian's dream.

1 pound black beans (turtle beans)
2 tablespoons salt
½ pound onions, diced
½ pound green peppers, diced
½ cup olive oil
5 cloves garlic, peeled
2 teaspoons cumin seed
2 tablespoons oregano
¼ cup white vinegar
1 hard-cooked egg, finely chopped

Wash the beans in cold water, place them in a 6-quart soup pot with enough water to cover, and bring them to a boil. Boil for a few minutes, then take the pot off the heat and allow the beans to soak for 1 hour. Add the salt and simmer the beans, partially covered, for 1½ hours until they are very tender.

Sauté the onions and green pepper in the oil until the onions are lightly browned. Crush the garlic, cumin and oregano in a mortar with a pestle, or mince the garlic and crush it in a small bowl with the cumin and oregano. Stir in the vinegar.

Add the seasoning mixture to the sautéed onions and green pepper and cook together on low heat for 5 minutes. Stir this into the black beans and simmer for 10 minutes, stirring occasionally until almost all the liquid has been absorbed. Put half the mixture through a food mill or puree in a food processor; leave the remainder whole.

Garnish with the hard-cooked egg and serve hot with fluffy steamed rice.

Beans Western-Style

1 pound dried kidney or pinto beans
2 medium-size onions, finely chopped
1 tablespoon finely chopped garlic
4 medium-size fully ripened tomatoes, peeled or diced (or substitute 2 cups canned)
2 medium-size red or green bell peppers, diced
½ teaspoon cumin
1 hot chili pepper, seeded and chopped (or 1 teaspoon chili powder, to taste)
2 tablespoons wine vinegar
2 tablespoons olive oil
Salt and pepper to taste

Soak the beans overnight in cold water or follow the directions on the package. Drain and simmer the beans in at least 3 or 4 inches of water for about 1 hour. Drain and reserve the liquid.

Preheat the oven to 325 degrees. Put the beans in a casserole with the remaining ingredients. Cover and bake for 2 hours. Add the reserved liquid if necessary. Adjust the seasonings. Serve with toasted crusty bread or tortillas.

NOTE: Cooking time for dried beans varies with the length of time the beans have been stored. Beans which have been dried and stored for 1 month will cook faster and absorb less liquid than those which have been stored for a year.

Dried Limas in Broth

2 cups (1 pound) dried limas
2 quarts chicken broth
1 onion, diced
2 ribs celery, diced
1 carrot, diced
Salt and pepper
2 tablespoons finely chopped parsley

Wash the beans in cold water.

There are 2 ways to prepare dried beans for cooking. You can presoak the beans overnight in 2 quarts of water; this is an age-old method. Or you can cover the beans with water in a 4- to 6-quart saucepan, bring the water to a boil, cover, and boil for 3 or 4 minutes. Turn off the heat and allow the beans to soak for 1 hour. They are now ready to be cooked.

Drain the soaked or cooked beans and add the chicken broth, onion, celery and carrots. Cover and simmer for 1 hour. Adjust the seasoning. (The flavor will depend greatly on the basic flavor of the chicken broth—homemade broth will taste better than canned.)

Drain and serve, with a sprinkling of parsley, as an accompaniment to chicken or duck.

NOTE: The cooking liquid can be a fine base for the next day's soup or stew, or it can be frozen for future use.

Beets

Beets can become two vegetables if they are bought fresh with the greens attached. If you are buying beets with the greens, cut the greens a few inches above the crown as they tend to bleed and lose color if they are cut close to the root.

The beet greens can be prepared in the same manner as collards and kale.

Swiss chard is in the beet family but it is a variety grown for the stalk and leaves, never developing a root.

Beets Vermont-Style

2 bunches (about 8) beets
½ teaspoon salt
1 tablespoon lemon juice
1 tablespoon butter
2 tablespoons maple syrup
1 tablespoon wine vinegar
¼ cup sour cream

Put the beets in boiling water to cover. Add the salt and lemon juice. Cover the pot and simmer for 15 to 20 minutes (cooking time depends on the size and maturity of the beets). Drain and allow the beets to cool or rinse them in cold water. Rub the skin off with your hands, trim the roots and slice the beets.

Heat the beets with the butter, maple syrup and wine vinegar. Serve very hot with a dab of sour cream.

NOTE: Beets may be baked. Brush them lightly with oil and bake at 350 degrees until they are tender (45 minutes to 1 hour).

Julienned beets and Belgian endive make a classic salad. Serve it as a first course with a mustard vinaigrette dressing.

Broccoli

Broccoli is a year-round favorite, readily available and generally not too expensive. Its relative, the cauliflower, is now available in a fashionable shade of purple. When it is cooked, the purple turns to green and the vegetable resembles broccoli, although it is slightly milder in flavor. These vegetables are delicious in a béchamel or cheese sauce.

Broccoli in Garlic Breadcrumbs

Serves 4-6

1 bunch broccoli
1½ teaspoons salt
2 tablespoons butter
1 teaspoon finely chopped garlic
½ cup breadcrumbs
1 teaspoon marjoram
¼ teaspoon pepper

Trim the ends of the broccoli and peel the heavy stems lightly, as you would asparagus. Slit the stem lengthwise to make the broccoli cook faster. Put the broccoli in a saucepan with 4 quarts boiling water and 1 teaspoon salt and cook over high heat. When the water returns to a boil, time the cooking for about 4 minutes or until the broccoli has reached the desired state of doneness. Drain.

In the meantime heat the butter in a large skillet. Add the garlic and cook for 1 or 2 minutes. Add the remaining ingredients and stir until the breadcrumbs are toasted.

Put the broccoli in a serving dish and sprinkle the breadcrumb mixture on top.

NOTE: Broccoli may be blanched in boiling water for 1 minute, then sautéed in olive oil and garlic to complete cooking. Or it may be stir-fried, in the manner described for Bean Sprouts. Leftover broccoli is good served hot with a dash of vinegar or cold in a tossed salad.

Broccoli-rabe

Broccoli-rabe is a market name for rapi or, in Italian, *broccoli di rapa*. This is a strong, assertive vegetable and it goes well with pasta, a perfect combination for a meatless meal.

Broccoli-rabe with Spaghetti

Serves 4

2-3 pounds broccoli-rabe
1 pound spaghetti or fettucini
½ cup olive oil
1 tablespoon finely chopped garlic
½ cup grated Parmesan cheese
¼ teaspoon red pepper flakes
Salt and pepper to taste

Wash the broccoli-rabe; trim off the tough ends and cut the stems into 3- or 4-inch pieces. Place a serving bowl in a very low oven to warm.

Boil 6 quarts of salted water in a large pot. Add the spaghetti and cover until the water returns to a boil. Uncover and stir to be sure all the strands are separated. Boil, uncovered, for 3 to 10 minutes, depending on personal taste and the freshness of the pasta. Add the broccoli-rabe 3 minutes before the pasta is finished.

In a separate skillet, heat the oil and sauté the garlic until it is glazed. Drain the pasta and broccoli and put it in the prewarmed bowl. Add the oil, garlic, cheese and red pepper, toss well, and add the salt and pepper to taste. Serve immediately.

Brussels Sprouts

It was only a few years ago that I first encountered brussels sprouts in their growing state. They were so attractively clustered, climbing on a thick stalk, that I used them as a Thanksgiving centerpiece that year. Tiny and fresh, raw brussels sprouts are delicious to nibble. If you must buy them packaged in boxes, be careful to avoid yellow leaves and blemishes.

To prepare brussels sprouts, cut off the ends, snap off the outer leaves, and wash well. They may harbor tiny insects; soak them if necessary. Try to avoid overcooking, as it makes the sprouts mushy.

Creamy Brussels Sprouts

Serves 4-6

1 pound brussels sprouts
1 egg
1 tablespoon lemon juice
¼ cup heavy cream
Salt and pepper to taste

Cut off the ends of the brussels sprouts and discard them. Wash the sprouts well and cook, uncovered, in boiling salted water for 5 to 7 minutes. Drain.

Beat the egg with the lemon juice, add the cream, and stir into the brussels sprouts. Warm through over medium heat. Adjust the seasoning and serve immediately.

Brussels Sprouts with Sherry Vinegar

Serves 4-6

1 pound brussels sprouts
1 tablespoon sherry vinegar
1 tablespoon butter or oil
Dash of nutmeg
Dash of black pepper

Cut off the ends and wash the brussels sprouts well. Cook, uncovered, in boiling salted water for 5 to 7 minutes. Drain. Season with the vinegar, butter, nutmeg and pepper.

Brussels Sprouts with Chestnuts

Serves 4-6

1 pound brussels sprouts
½ pound Fresh Roasted Chestnuts
   (recipe on page 40)
2 tablespoons butter
Salt and pepper to taste

Cut off the ends and wash the brussels sprouts well. Cook, uncovered, in boiling water for 5 to 7 minutes. Drain.
Add the chestnuts and butter. Adjust the seasoning.

Cabbage

Cabbage has a long line of cousins: brussels sprouts, broccoli, cauliflower, kale, kohlrabi and a few other less familiar ones. Cabbage itself grows in shades of white, green and red, and in round, flat, cone-like, curly, plain and leafy heads. The soil of the world is its bed, and the kitchens of the world have created wonders with this most ordinary, nutritious and economical vegetable.

Stuffed Cabbage with Lemon and Garlic   Serves 6

One of my favorite hors d'oeuvres, hot or cold, is this Near Eastern dish. You can make an equally delicious vegetarian version by substituting 1 cup each cracked wheat (bulgur) and raisins for the meat.

1 pound ground beef
¾ cup cooked rice
1 tablespoon plus 1 teaspoon salt
½ teaspoon pepper
**1 large cabbage (preferably with
  very green leaves)**
¼ cup lemon juice
¼ cup finely chopped garlic
¼ pound butter

Mix together the beef, rice, 1 teaspoon salt and the pepper and set the mixture aside for the stuffing.

Turn the cabbage upside down and cut out the core to form a cavity. Loosen any leaves that cling to the core.

Immerse the cabbage in boiling water to which 1 tablespoon salt has been added and simmer for 4 or 5 minutes, covered. Use a long-tined fork to remove 1 or 2 leaves. If they are pliable enough to roll, remove more. The inside of the cabbage takes longer to cook. Continue to remove the leaves as they become tender. Cut large leaves in half so that the maximum length of each leaf is about 3 inches. Dry them on absorbent paper.

Place half a teaspoon of the meat and rice mixture along the middle of each leaf and roll it up to form a small tube. The tubes should be loosely rolled to allow room for the rice to expand. Place the rolls in neat rows on the bottom of a 6-quart Dutch oven or heavy-duty saucepan. The next row is placed directly on top at a right angle to the bottom row. Repeat until all the stuffing mixture is used. Add the lemon juice and garlic, and dot with pieces of butter. Cover and cook over moderate heat for 1 hour.

NOTE: Another way to wilt cabbage leaves is to freeze the cabbage for at least 24 hours, then defrost it. The leaves will separate and be soft enough to roll and fold.

Chinese Cabbage with Sesame Seeds

Serves 4

Chinese cabbage has a mild flavor. It stores extremely well in the refrigerator and is a good staple for use in mixed salads as well as slaws, American or Chinese. Cook it like cabbage or stir-fry it Chinese-style.

3 tablespoons vegetable or
   peanut oil
¼ cup sesame seeds
2 slices ginger root
4 cups diced Chinese cabbage
1 cup diced fresh mushrooms
1 tablespoon soy sauce
1 tablespoon sherry or dry vermouth
¼ cup chicken broth
Salt and pepper to taste
1 teaspoon sesame oil

Warm a serving platter in a low oven.

Heat 1 tablespoon oil in a wok or skillet. Add the sesame seeds, stir to coat and toast them evenly, and then put them on a plate.

Add 1 tablespoon oil to the wok or skillet. Heat, and add the ginger-root slices. Brown them, then add the cabbage and stir-fry. Put the cabbage on the warm platter.

Heat 1 tablespoon of oil in the skillet and add the mushrooms. Cook for 1 minute. Add the cabbage to the mushrooms and cook for another minute. Add all the remaining ingredients except the sesame oil. Stir-fry on high heat for 1 minute. Adjust the seasoning with salt and pepper, sprinkle with sesame oil, and serve immediately on the warm platter.

Sweet-and-Sour Red Cabbage

2 pounds red cabbage
2 tablespoons butter or oil
2 medium-size onions, sliced
2 apples, peeled and diced
2 tablespoons lemon juice
2 teaspoons salt
2 tablespoons flour
3 tablespoons sugar
4 tablespoons vinegar

Trim off the bottom of the cabbage and discard it. Cut the cabbage in half and wash it well. Shred it by hand with a chef's knife or in a processor. Heat the butter or oil in a Dutch oven or stewpot with a tight-fitting lid, and cook the onion until it is just glazed and lightly browned. Add the cabbage, apples, lemon juice and salt. Cook, firmly covered, for 20 minutes. Make a paste of flour, sugar and vinegar. Add it to the cabbage; cover and cook for 20 to 30 minutes more. Adjust the seasoning to your taste—some people like more tartness, some more sweetness and some more saltiness.

NOTE: This dish may be made and refrigerated for up to 5 days, or frozen for up to 3 months. It is an excellent accompaniment served with game, pork, ham or smoked sausage.

Cabbage and Noodle Strudel

Serves 8

The filo dough used in this Hungarian strudel can be found in most specialty stores and even some supermarkets.

2-pound cabbage
½ pound medium-sized broad egg noodles, cooked
6 tablespoons clarified butter or oil
2 medium-size onions, diced
1 tablespoon finely chopped parsley
½ teaspoon paprika
Salt and pepper
6 sheets filo pastry
¼ cup breadcrumbs

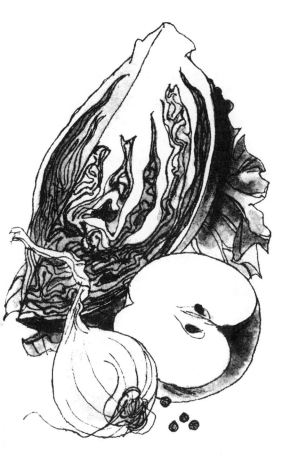

Preheat the oven to 350 degrees.

Cook the cabbage as for Sweet-and-Sour Red Cabbage, mix it with the noodles, and drain.

Heat 2 tablespoons butter in a large skillet and sauté the onions until they have a touch of brown. Add the cabbage and noodles to the skillet, stir, and cook for 3 minutes. Turn into a bowl and add the parsley and paprika. Stir well and adjust the seasoning. Refrigerate.

When the mixture is cold, prepare the pastry. Have a pastry brush handy to spread the clarified butter.

Spread 1 sheet of filo pastry on an 11-by-15-inch jelly-roll pan. Brush it with butter and immediately place another sheet on top. Brush it with butter and sprinkle it with about 1 tablespoon of breadcrumbs. Repeat with the remaining 4 sheets. Spread the cold cabbage and noodles across the length of the sixth sheet, leaving a 2-inch border of pastry across the bottom and up the sides. Bring the bottom border up and the side borders in to enclose the filling. Roll up the strudel and move it to the center of the pan*. Brush the top with clarified butter and bake for 30 minutes.

NOTE: The uncooked strudel can be refrigerated overnight or wrapped well and frozen.

Carrots

Carrots should be sweet; your best bet is to buy them fresh, in leafy bunches, when possible. They store well and are an excellent source of vitamin A. Raw carrots make a healthy, crunchy snack; cooked, they are a prime ingredient in soups, stocks and stews.

Glazed Carrots

Serves 4

6 carrots (1 pound)
1 tablespoon butter
1 teaspoon sugar

Scrub or peel the carrots and cut them into 1-inch chunks. Using a sharp paring knife, cut and turn the pieces into balls or tiny carrot shapes.

Place the carrots in a saucepan with 1 cup of salted water to cover. Cut a round of wax paper to fit closely on top, and simmer for 5 to 7 minutes; the wax paper will prevent the steam from evaporating, allowing the carrots to cook more quickly. Remove the wax paper and add the butter and sugar. Boil until the liquid evaporates and the carrots are lightly browned.

Floridian Carrots

Serves 4

Friends in Florida suggested the happy combination of carrots and fresh citrus fruits; mint adds a refreshing touch.

6 carrots (1 pound)
½ cup fresh orange juice
1 tablespoon fresh lemon juice
1 wedge of lemon
Salt and pepper to taste
1 tablespoon wine vinegar
1 teaspoon dried mint (or 3 to
   4 fresh leaves, slivered)

Scrub or lightly peel the carrots and cut them into rounds. Combine the carrots, orange and lemon juice and the lemon wedge in a saucepan. Add sufficient water to cover the carrots. Simmer, covered, for 5 to 7 minutes.

Pour off the liquid (reserving it for soup stock or other uses) and discard the lemon wedge. Season the carrots with the salt, pepper and wine vinegar. Toss with the mint and serve.

Cauliflower

Cauliflower should be white, unblemished and tightly bunched, with fresh green leaves hugging its round shape. Small insects may nest in cauliflower; if you are cooking the head whole, soak it first in cold water with 1 tablespoon lemon juice.

Boiled Whole Cauliflower

Serves 4-6

1 cauliflower
1 tablespoon salt
2 tablespoons lemon juice

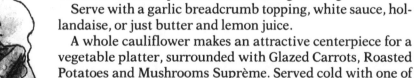

Boil enough water to cover the entire head. Add the salt and lemon juice, immerse the cauliflower, cover, and simmer for about 20 minutes. (Timing depends on the size; most heads take anywhere from 15 to 30 minutes. Remember that cauliflower cut into florets cooks in a much shorter time; allow about 10 to 12 minutes.) White vegetables remain whiter if the saucepan is covered during cooking.

Serve with a garlic breadcrumb topping, white sauce, hollandaise, or just butter and lemon juice.

A whole cauliflower makes an attractive centerpiece for a vegetable platter, surrounded with Glazed Carrots, Roasted Potatoes and Mushrooms Suprème. Served cold with one of the cold sauces described at the end of this book, it can be a refreshing luncheon vegetable.

NOTE: Cauliflower can be steamed but should be cut into florets first.

Celeriac

Celeriac is a particular personal favorite; some call it celery root or knob celery. Whatever name it goes by, it is a knobby, ugly, most earthy-looking root. Celeriac can be refrigerated for more than a week and adds an assertive, interesting celery flavor when added to chicken broth and purees. Be sure to toss it with fresh lemon juice after it is peeled because celeriac discolors quickly when exposed to the air.

Celeriac in Broth
Serves 4

1 large celeriac
2 onions, cut into quarters
1 tablespoon lemon juice
1 cup chicken broth
2 tablespoons butter or heavy cream
Salt and pepper to taste

Wash the celeriac; peel it with a sharp paring knife and cut it into small pieces. Place the celeriac, onions, lemon juice and broth in a saucepan, cover, and simmer for 5 to 6 minutes or until it is tender. Uncover and boil until the liquid reduces to half the original quantity, then add the butter or cream. Season with the salt and pepper.

NOTE: The butter or cream may, of course, be omitted if you are watching calories.

Celery

Celery really needs no introduction. It is equally invaluable to serious cooks and to dieters. Ribs of raw celery are served stuffed as hors d'oeuvres or with dips before a meal; braised celery is a superb hot dish; and it is as useful as carrots as an all-purpose, aromatic flavoring vegetable.

Braised Celery with Scallions

Serves 4-6

2 bunches celery
2 bunches scallions
½ teaspoon tarragon
1 cup hot chicken broth
2 tablespoons butter
Salt and pepper to taste

Remove the tough outer ribs of the celery; save them for use in a soup or stew. Wash the celery well. Cut each stalk into quarters, leaving some of the tender leaves. Wash the scallions and trim the green ends neatly to make uniform lengths. The celery and scallions may also be cut into julienne strips, if you prefer.

Bring 3 quarts of water to a boil. Add and cook the celery for 3 or 4 minutes, then put it in a 2-quart casserole. Blanch the scallions for 30 seconds in the same boiling water.

Put the scallions in the casserole with the cooked celery and tarragon and add the broth. Cover and bake for 45 minutes. Dot with butter and serve.

NOTE: Cooked celery is ideal served with a béchamel or cheese sauce.

Chestnuts

Chestnuts are a seasonal treat, but cooking them can be a chore. Some years back I was taught how to prepare fresh roasted chestnuts—an Italian family technique. It is easy and it works!

Fresh Roasted Chestnuts
Serves 4

Preheat the oven to 450 degrees. Oil a jelly-roll pan. Wash 1 pound of chestnuts. Using a small, sharp paring knife, cut through a tiny sliver of shell—about ¼ inch—on the flat side of the chestnut, barely penetrating the flesh. Place them in the prepared pan and bake 10 to 15 minutes.

Test for doneness by placing one chestnut on a dishcloth, folding the cloth over, and pressing to crush the shell. If the shell comes off easily, the chestnuts are ready. Put all the chestnuts in the cloth and press them to crack the shells. They are more easily shelled while they are hot, so keep them covered as you work. (Keep a bowl of ice water handy and dip your fingers in the water as you proceed.) If some nuts prove stubborn, place them in the oven again for a few minutes.

The chestnuts may now be used in stuffings and as accompaniments for other dishes.

For use in purees and desserts, boil the shelled chestnuts in water, broth or milk until they are soft.

Collards

Collard greens are a humble but very important vegetable in the South. Members of the kale family, collards are hardy winter vegetables that are low in calories and high in vitamins. Greens, as they are called in the South, make good eating with a touch of bacon or salt pork.

Collard Greens and Bacon
Serves 4

2-3 pounds collards
½ pound bacon, diced
¼ teaspoon red pepper flakes
Salt and pepper

Wash the collards well in water. Trim off the tough stems and shred the remainder. Blanch the greens in 4 quarts of salted boiling water. Boil for 2 to 3 minutes, then drain well.

Render the bacon in a skillet until it is crisp and pour off most of the fat. Add the greens and seasonings to the skillet and stir-fry for 2 to 3 minutes, then cover, and cook for 5 minutes.

Serve with butter if you wish.

Corn

If you are lucky enough to grow your own corn, pick it moments before cooking—sweet, juicy, fresh corn is an incomparable treat. A local farm stand will have to suffice if you do not grow your own crop. In either case, husk the corn only when you are ready to cook it.

Corn Stew

Serves 4

Even if your corn is a day or two old, do not discard it; stew it instead.

8 ears corn
4 tablespoons butter
1 onion, chopped
½ cup chopped sweet green pepper
½ cup chopped sweet red pepper
½ cup light cream
2 tablespoons finely chopped parsley
Salt and pepper to taste

There is a special tool on the market for cutting kernels off the cob, but any small, sharp knife will do. Be sure to save all the milky juices that ooze out of the cob. Set the corn aside.

Melt the butter in a saucepan. Stir in the onion and cook it until it is golden and glazed. Add the green and red peppers and stir for 2 to 3 minutes; then add the corn kernels. Turn the heat up and stir well for 2 minutes. Add the light cream, parsley, salt and pepper, then cover, and simmer for 45 minutes. * This stew can also be baked in a covered casserole at 350 degrees for 1 hour.

NOTE: Prepare a day ahead or freeze for future use.

The Pennsylvania Dutch use dried corn; reconstitute it as you would dried beans and then follow the recipe. It is delicious.

Cucumber

Cucumber is really a fruit, although we generally treat it as a salad vegetable or use it in pickling. The long seedless varieties, the kirbys, and the lemon cucumber work especially well for Herbed Cucumbers.

Herbed Cucumbers
Serves 4

4 large cucumbers (about 2 pounds)
2 tablespoons lemon juice
1 teaspoon kosher salt
¼ teaspoon sugar
1 tablespoon butter or oil
¼ cup minced shallots
¼ cup chicken broth
1 cup cream
2 tablespoons finely chopped parsley
2 teaspoons dried thyme

Peel the cucumbers, halve them lengthwise, and scoop out the seeds with a spoon. Cut them into slices or strips, then marinate them in the lemon juice, salt and sugar for about 15 minutes. Drain well and dry them with paper toweling.

Heat the butter or oil in a skillet or saucepan. Add the shallots and sauté for 2 to 3 minutes to glaze them. Add the cucumbers and chicken broth. Cook the cucumbers until the broth has evaporated—about 5 minutes—shaking the pan and stirring occasionally.

Meanwhile, simmer the cream with the dill, parsley and thyme until the liquid is reduced by half. Add the cream to the cooked cucumbers and serve immediately.

Eggplant

The eggplant is a beautiful vegetable, with its sleek, leathery skin. Although usually dark purple to black, there are also white- and yellow-skinned varieties. There is much controversy over how to choose an eggplant. Some say it should weigh "light" for its size; some say choose a female, although I have been told by a botanist that there is no such thing. My advice is to choose firm, shiny eggplants with no sponginess or brown spots.

Opinion also differs on whether to salt and weight down slices of eggplant to release water and bitterness before cooking. After years of advising students to do so, I stopped recommending this procedure when I discovered that it made little difference.

Eggplants are as much a staple in my house as onions and carrots. A few pieces of eggplant stewed with onions, mushrooms and tomatoes make a good side dish with a simple fish, meat or pasta entree. A slice of eggplant can be grilled with a lamb chop, hamburger or small steak.

Eggplant Caviar

Serves 4-6

This recipe hardly resembles caviar in taste, but the presence of the seeds gives it a similar appearance. It is a particular family favorite. Tasty, economical and low in calories, it can be kept for a week or more in the refrigerator.

1 eggplant (about ½ pound)
1 small green pepper
1 small red pepper
1 hot red pepper (optional)
1 small onion, peeled
1 clove garlic, peeled
2 tablespoons wine vinegar or
   lemon juice
2 tablespoons olive oil
⅛ teaspoon red pepper flakes

If you have a gas range, char and soften the eggplant and peppers directly on the burner, turning the vegetables to cook them evenly. If you have an electric stove, broil the eggplant and peppers 4 to 5 inches below the element. Puncture the skin of the eggplant in 4 or 5 places. Put the eggplant and peppers on a baking tin and place them under the broiler for about 20 minutes, turning occasionally. The skin should be charred and the eggplant soft when touched or pierced with a fork.

Remove the eggplant and peppers to a paper bag. Seal it on top and allow the vegetables to cool. Remove the skin from the eggplant and the peppers, and clean out the seeds of the peppers.

Chop the onion and garlic finely in a processor. Add the eggplant and peppers. Turn the machine on and off just to chop the eggplant roughly; do not make a mush. (Sometimes I do the chopping by hand with a chef's knife.) Turn into a bowl and season with the vinegar, oil, pepper flakes, and salt and pepper to taste.

NOTE: For a spicy touch, char a tiny hot pepper with the sweet ones.

Rolled Eggplant

2-pound eggplant
2-3 cups peanut oil for frying
1 cup flour
½ teaspoon salt
½ teaspoon pepper
1 pound cottage cheese or ricotta
¼ pound sharp cheddar cheese,
**   grated**
1 tablespoon finely chopped parsley
1 teaspoon marjoram
2 tablespoons breadcrumbs

Preheat the oven to 400 degrees.

Cut the eggplant into ¼-inch slices.

Pour the oil into a deep fryer or skillet and set it on medium heat until you are ready to fry. Spread out paper towels for blotting. Mix the flour with the salt and ¼ teaspoon of pepper and spread it on a sheet of wax paper. Dredge the eggplant slices in flour, one at a time.

Raise the heat of the oil to frying point (375 degrees). Fry 2 or 3 pieces of eggplant at a time and blot them on paper towels. Repeat until all the slices are fried. Eggplant can also be sprinkled with oil and broiled.

Mix together the cheeses, parsley, marjoram and remaining pepper. Divide the filling evenly among the slices of eggplant and roll each slice so that the sides turn up around the filling. Place the rolls in a 9-by-13-inch ovenproof dish and sprinkle them with the breadcrumbs. * Bake, uncovered, for 10 minutes just before serving.

NOTE: Serve as a light main course with Fresh Tomato Sauce (recipe on page 83). Tossed salad, crusty bread and a California red table wine complete the menu.

Eggplant Parmigiana

Serves 4

2-pound eggplant
2 eggs
2 tablespoons water
2 tablespoons flour
1 teaspoon salt
½ teaspoon pepper
1 cup breadcrumbs
2-3 cups vegetable or peanut oil
2 cups marinara or favorite tomato
   sauce
2 tablespoons finely chopped parsley
½ pound mozzarella cheese, thinly
   sliced
¼ pound Parmesan cheese, grated

Preheat the oven to 425 degrees.

Peel the eggplant if the skin is heavy and tough. Slice it horizontally into very thin slices. Beat the eggs with the water, flour, salt and pepper. Spread the breadcrumbs on a sheet of wax paper and lay out paper towels for blotting.

Heat the oil in a deep skillet to 375 degrees or hot enough to lightly toast a cube of bread in 30 seconds. Dip each eggplant slice in the egg mixture, and then in the breadcrumbs. Fry for 1 minute on each side. Fry only 2 or 3 slices at a time to avoid lowering the temperature of the oil. Blot the fried slices on the paper towels.

In an 11-by-15-inch jelly-roll pan, sandwich 2 slices together to form a double layer. Spread tomato sauce on top of each double layer and sprinkle it with the parsley. Bake for 5 to 7 minutes.

Place a slice of mozzarella and a sprinkling of Parmesan on each layer, using half the Parmesan. Bake for 1 minute more or until the cheeses melt and bubble. Serve immediately with the remaining Parmesan on the side.

NOTE: Four or 5 very thin slices of eggplant, sliced lengthwise, can constitute a meal, served with a salad, crusty Italian bread and red wine.

Fennel

Fennel is often called by its Italian name, *finocchio*. It has feathery leaves and flavorful seeds which are used in fish soups, stews, charcoal grilling and even in cookies and breads. Although the stalks rather resemble celery, it is the bulb or bottom that is most often used as a vegetable. It can be eaten raw in salads, or cooked and served hot or cold.

Crusty Batter-Fried Fennel   *Serves 4*

I have a fond recollection of the crisp batter-fried fennel I first tasted in Naples many years ago.

3-4 stalks fennel
1⅓ cups flour
2 eggs
⅓ cup milk
1 teaspoon salt
¼ teaspoon pepper
1 cup breadcrumbs
3 cups vegetable or peanut oil

Cut off the feathery leaves of the fennel and save them for flavoring soups or fish. Wash and cut the bulbs into quarters. Boil enough salted water to cover the fennel. Parboil the pieces for 3 minutes, then rinse them under cold water and dry them thoroughly.

Combine ⅓ cup of flour with the eggs, milk, salt and pepper to make a batter. Spread the remaining flour on a sheet of wax paper and spread the breadcrumbs on another sheet. Roll each piece of fennel in flour, then dip it in the batter, and then roll it in the breadcrumbs. Set it aside on a dish until you are ready to cook it.*

Heat the oil in a deep-fryer to 375 degrees, or until a cube of white bread toasts in 30 seconds. Fry a few pieces of fennel at a time, removing each piece to paper towels to drain.

The fried fennel can be kept warm in a 250-degree oven for 30 minutes, but it is better served immediately.

Jerusalem Artichokes

The Jerusalem artichoke is not from Jerusalem, nor is it an artichoke; it is a native North American tuber that somewhat resembles a potato but has a crisp texture and a sweeter taste. In hues of brown, yellow and purple, it is rather knobby in appearance and therefore easier to scrub than to peel. (The French name for this vegetable sounds wonderfully exotic: *topinambour*.)

Jerusalem Artichokes in Cream
Serves 4

1 pound Jerusalem artichokes
1 small onion, coarsely chopped
1 pound mushrooms, quartered
½ cup water
1 teaspoon salt
2 tablespoons lemon juice
1 sprig each, thyme and parsley
½ cup heavy cream
1 tablespoon flour
½ cup sour cream
¼ teaspoon pepper
Pinch cayenne

Scrub the vegetables with a stiff brush. Cut them into chunks.

Combine the Jerusalem artichokes, onion, mushrooms, water, ½ teaspoon salt, lemon juice, thyme and parsley in a saucepan. Cover and bring to a boil. Reduce the heat and cook 3 to 4 minutes, until the Jerusalem artichokes are tender; drain off all the liquid.

Whisk the heavy cream into the flour, a tablespoon at a time, and beat until the cream is smooth. Blend in the sour cream, the remaining salt and seasonings.

Discard the thyme and parsley. Pour the cream mixture into the saucepan with the artichokes, onions and mushrooms. * Bring to a boil and cook, uncovered, for a few minutes. Serve immediately.

Kale

Kale is a dark, leafy, coarse green variety of cabbage. In spite of instructions to the contrary in many recipes, I prefer not to cook it too long, so that it keeps its bite and texture.

Chopped Kale

1 bunch kale
1 cup light cream
1 tablespoon finely chopped garlic
   or ginger root
½ onion, studded with bay leaf
   and cloves
Salt and pepper to taste

Discard the stems and wash the kale well. Boil 2 quarts of water and add the kale. Cook it for 7 minutes after the water returns to a boil. Drain off the water and press the moisture out of the kale. Chop it coarsely on a board.

Heat the cream, garlic (or ginger) and onion, and boil them to reduce the liquid by half. Discard the onion and add the kale. Season with salt and pepper, heat, and serve.

NOTE: Cooked kale can be seasoned simply with diced bacon or sautéed garlic, omitting the cream.

Kohlrabi

Kohlrabi is a forgotten vegetable. Although it is a member of the cabbage family, it is much more gentle in flavor. The stems of kohlrabi are edible, but their flavor is usually too strong for my taste. Kohlrabi resembles a turnip in shape, but it is not a root vegetable. Eat kohlrabi raw for its crispness or serve it cooked as an alternative to cabbage.

Kohlrabi

4-6 kohlrabi
Salt and pepper to taste
1 teaspoon dried savory
1 tablespoon butter or oil (optional)

Cut off the stems of the kohlrabi and peel the bulblike portion. (If it is young and fresh from the garden, it can be cooked peel and all.) Slice or dice the kohlrabi as you wish. Put it in a saucepan, cover it with salted water, and cook, covered, for 6 minutes, or until it is tender.

Drain off the liquid; reserve it for vegetable broths. Season it with the salt, pepper and savory. Butter or oil may be added.

Mushrooms

Mushrooms are sold year round, but they are best in the cooler months. They have a short shelf life, so be sure to select the ones that are firm, with tightly closed caps. When the mushrooms are no longer fresh, the caps will open to show the gills underneath. Older ones are usable in sauces or stews, but they are not as flavorful or handsome as the very fresh ones. Fresh mushrooms will keep well in the refrigerator for 7 days in an ordinary paper bag. Do not wrap them in plastic. Before cooking, wipe the mushrooms clean; if they are very dirty, gently wash and dry them.

Mushrooms Suprème

1 pound mushrooms
2 tablespoons butter
¼ cup Cognac
½ cup heavy cream
Salt and pepper to taste
2 tablespoons finely chopped parsley
½ teaspoon finely chopped fresh
tarragon (optional)

Slice off the ends of the mushroom stems; save them for soups and stews. Slice the mushrooms.

Heat the butter in a skillet, add the mushrooms, and sauté them over high heat, shaking the pan to brown them evenly. Add the Cognac and continue to cook until it evaporates. Add the cream and boil to reduce by half. Add the seasonings and the herbs and serve as a main course for lunch or as a side dish.

Duxelles

There are several possible derivations for the term duxelles, *which denotes a hash of minced, sautéed mushrooms. Some say it originated in Uxel, a small town in France; others that it was created by the great chef La Varenne, who was in the service of the Marquis d'Uxelles. Whatever its origin, it is a standard and outstanding preparation used by all knowledgeable cooks.*

1 pound mushrooms
¼ cup finely chopped shallots
or onions
4 tablespoons butter
Salt and pepper to taste

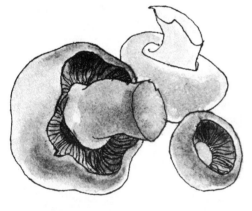

Chop the mushrooms finely. Heat a heavy skillet and sauté the shallots or onions in the butter until they wilt. Add the mushrooms and sauté them until all the moisture evaporates. Stir occasionally to prevent them from burning. Season them with the salt and pepper but use a light hand if the dish is to be added to another food that is already seasoned.

Cooked duxelles can be stored in the refrigerator or freezer. Use ice-cube trays for small amounts, or divide the duxelles among several small plastic containers or bags.

Duxelles on Toast

Serves 4-6

For an elegant brunch or luncheon, serve a platter of these open-faced sandwiches to accompany omelettes or a soup.

1 duxelles recipe
1 teaspoon tarragon
1 tablespoon finely chopped parsley
1 tablespoon sherry
2 tablespoons heavy cream
Pinch cayenne
4-6 slices white or French bread
2 ounces Gruyère cheese, thinly
sliced

Mix the duxelles with the herbs, sherry, cream and cayenne. Taste and adjust the seasoning. Remove the crusts if you are using white bread; if you are using French bread, leave the crusts. Toast one side of the bread under the broiler. Spread the duxelles on the untoasted side of the bread and top them with the cheese.

Bake the toast in a hot oven for 5 minutes until the cheese has melted, or place it under the broiler, being careful not to let it burn. Cut it into bite-sized squares or triangles, or serve a whole slice on each plate along with a knife and fork.

Mushrooms and Caviar

This elegant mushroom dish was inspired by a similar presentation we enjoyed on a trip to Denmark.

1 bunch fresh parsley, stemmed
1 cup sour cream
2-ounce jar red caviar
2-4 tablespoons butter
1 pound large mushrooms, stems removed

Use a 12-inch round serving platter and an attractive serving bowl that will fit in the center of the platter leaving a 3-inch border all around.

Wash the parsley, dry it very well, and refrigerate it in a covered container to crisp it.

Lightly blend the sour cream and caviar and spoon them into the serving bowl. Place the parsley around the bowl to fill the border completely.

Heat a skillet until it is hot enough for a drop of butter to sizzle immediately. Add the remainder of the butter and sauté the mushrooms on high heat for no more than 2 minutes, allowing them to remain slightly firm.

Place the mushrooms on the bed of parsley around the bowl of caviar cream. Season with the salt and pepper, and serve immediately. Guests may help themselves by topping the mushrooms with a dollop of the cream.

NOTE: If you have the occasion and the budget, serve the mushrooms with *crème fraîche*, fresh caviar and parsley that has been deep-fried in butter for just 10 seconds.

Onions

The onion family is a cook's treasure chest; so many foods are enhanced by the flavors of garlic, scallions, leeks and shallots. The onion itself is a staple that can be stored without refrigeration; it is always on hand when many fresh vegetables are out of season.

Baked Onions

Preheat the oven to 350 degrees.

Choose onions of uniform size, allowing 2 onions per person. Trim off both ends. Put the onions on a baking sheet and bake them 30 to 40 minutes, or until they are tender. Slip off the skins. Pass the butter, salt and pepper at the table. Nutmeg also goes very nicely with baked onions.

Stuffed Onions

Serves 4

4 large onions
2 slices bacon, diced
1 cup white or brown cooked rice
¼ cup raisins
¼ cup toasted pignolia nuts or
    diced blanched almonds
¼ teaspoon cinnamon
Salt and pepper to taste
½ cup chicken broth
½ cup breadcrumbs
1 tablespoon finely chopped parsley

Preheat the oven to 375 degrees.

Immerse the onions in salted boiling water and boil them for 7 to 8 minutes. Drain the onions and cool them. When they are cool enough to handle, remove the centers, using a small sharp knife and leave at least ½-inch of rim. Chop the scooped-out onion.

Fry the bacon until it is crisp. Add the chopped onion and sauté in the bacon fat until it is glazed. Stir in the rice and cook it for 1 minute, then remove the skillet from the heat. Add the raisins, nuts and cinnamon, and season with the salt and pepper.

Stuff the onions with the rice mixture. Place them in an 8-inch ovenproof dish and add the chicken broth. Cover the dish with aluminum foil and bake for 35 minutes. * Uncover and sprinkle the breadcrumbs on top. Bake, uncovered, for another 5 minutes. Garnish with the parsley and serve.

NOTE: This dish is equally good eaten at room temperature.

Parsnips

Many Americans are still unfamiliar with this vegetable. I myself started using parsnips only about five years ago; they have since become treasured friends in my kitchen.

Country Kitchen Parsnips

Serves 4

2 medium-size onions, sliced
6-8 parsnips (2 pounds)
2 tablespoons butter
½ cup chicken broth
½ cup heavy cream
½ teaspoon marjoram
1 tablespoon finely chopped parsley

Preheat the oven to 350 degrees.

Spread half of the onion slices over the bottom of a 1½-quart flameproof casserole.

Peel the parsnips and cut them in rounds or vertically in quarters. Cover them with salted water and boil for 5 minutes. Drain the liquid and reserve it for vegetable broth.

Add all the remaining ingredients to the parsnips and spoon the mixture on top of the onion slices in the casserole. Bake for 45 minutes.

Peppers

When I think of how nutritious red, green and yellow peppers are, I feel good about enjoying them so much. They are delicious eaten raw, but I find them even better charred and skinned. One of my Italian students was shocked to see me run a skinned pepper under water to remove the seeds. I have never committed that error again—the water drains off flavor, too!

The easiest way to skin peppers is to broil them at least four inches from the heat. Keep turning them until they are charred and soft. Place them in a paper bag to steam and cool off. Peel off the skins and remove the stem ends. Scrape out the seeds and pile the peppers into a jar with a sprinkling of olive oil. They can be refrigerated for a week or more.

Peppers are excellent by themselves or in interesting combinations, as an appetizer, a salad or a vegetable dish.

Conserve of Peppers and Anchovies

Serves 6-8

This recipe is good served cold on crusty bread or hot with a scaloppine of veal.

2 ounces anchovies (with oil)
2 pounds red and/or green peppers
½ cup olive oil
¼ cup finely chopped garlic
½ teaspoon pepper

Preheat the oven to 300 degrees.

Cut the anchovies into small pieces and put them in a baking dish large enough to hold the peppers.

Wash the peppers. Cut each pepper in half and discard the membranes and seeds. Cut the peppers into strips. Place all the ingredients in the baking dish with the anchovies and toss them to mix well.

Cover the baking dish with aluminum foil and bake for 45 minutes, stirring once or twice. Lower the oven temperature to 250 degrees and cook, uncovered, for 30 minutes more.* Serve warm or cold as a spread.

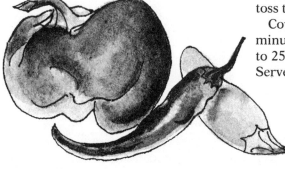

Stuffed Peppers

Serves 8

8 green peppers, each about
    5 inches long
1 cup breadcrumbs
½ cup finely chopped Italian parsley
13 oil-cured black olives, pitted and
    cut into small pieces
2 ounces canned anchovies in olive
    oil, cut into small pieces
1 teaspoon finely chopped garlic
¼ teaspoon oregano
¼ teaspoon black pepper
1 teaspoon grated Romano cheese
1 teaspoon white wine
4 tablespoons olive oil
⅓ cup cold water

Wash the peppers and dry them well. Cut out the stems, reserving them; halve the peppers and remove the seeds.

Place the breadcrumbs in a medium-size bowl and add all the other ingredients, reserving 2 tablespoons of the olive oil. Mix them well with a fork. Stuff the peppers with the mixture and replace the stems.

Heat the remaining olive oil in a large skillet and fry the peppers. Let them brown slowly on all sides, turning them with tongs. Be careful not to break the skins.

With a large spoon, lift the peppers out of the pan into a serving dish. Serve hot or at room temperature as an appetizer or side dish.

Plantains

The plantain is the "potato of the tropics," so widespread is its use there, but it is now becoming more readily available in the Northeast. Although it is a member of the banana family, it must be cooked to be edible. Like the banana, the plantain varies in color from green to yellow to black, each color indicating a different texture and therefore necessitating a different cooking technique. Plantains can be boiled, fried, sautéed or baked, and they may be served with fish, meat or poultry.

Baked Plantains with Rum
Serves 4

2 tablespoons butter
2 yellow (semiripe) plantains
½ pound onions, peeled and sliced
¼ cup breadcrumbs
Salt and pepper
¼ cup lime juice
½ cup rum

Preheat the oven to 350 degrees. Grease an 8-inch oven-proof dish with 1 tablespoon of butter.

Peel the plantains; cut them diagonally into 3-inch slices and then vertically in half. Immerse them in salted boiling water with the onions and cook, covered, for 3 to 4 minutes. Remove the plantains and the onions with a slotted spoon and dry them on paper towels.

Place the plantains and the onions in the buttered dish and sprinkle them with the lime juice. Dot them with the remaining butter, scatter the breadcrumbs over the surface and season with the salt and pepper. Bake, uncovered, for 10 minutes; add the rum and bake for 5 minutes more.

Serve with baked or broiled chicken or fish.

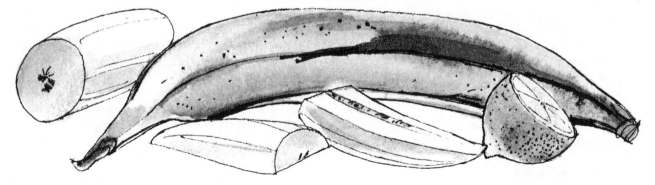

Potatoes

Dieting has consigned the marvelous potato—quite unfairly—to a low position on the "allowed" list of edibles. Actually, the potato not only compares favorably to other vegetables in terms of calories, but it is much higher in nutritive value than many. Although most people bake Idaho potatoes, this variety can be rather dry if not smothered in butter or cream. Try baking small, thin-skinned new potatoes at 425 degrees for 30 minutes. (Always prick potatoes with a fork in several places before baking them.)

Potato Pudding   *Serves 12*

4 tablespoons oil, clarified butter or chicken fat
2 pounds potatoes, 1 pound peeled and quartered and 1 pound peeled and left whole
2 small onions, peeled and quartered
½ cup cold water
½ cup boiling water
3 eggs, beaten
⅓ cup cracker meal, matzo meal or flour
1 teaspoon salt
½ teapoon pepper

Preheat the oven to 425 degrees.

Place 1 teaspoon oil or preferred fat in each well of a 12-cup muffin tin. Place the tin in the oven for 5 minutes.

Place the quartered potatoes, the onions and cold water into a processor and run it for 30 seconds, to chop the potatoes very finely without pureeing or liquifying them. Strain the potatoes, catching the liquid in a bowl. Let the liquid stand for a while and then pour off all the water in the bowl; there should be some potato starch clinging to the bottom. Grate the remaining potatoes by hand (I like the texture) and put them in a strainer. Pour the boiling water over them to help retain their color, and press out the liquid.

Mix the potatoes, eggs, cracker meal, salt and pepper in a bowl containing the potato starch and adjust the seasoning. Spoon the mixture into the heated muffin tin and bake for 30 minutes more. The puddings should come out of the tin easily. They are delicious accompaniments to roast veal, beef or chicken.

Potato Paprikash

This recipe is a family favorite, a hand-me-down from my grandmother.

3 tablespoons butter
¾ pound onions, sliced
½ pound green peppers, diced
1½ pounds potatoes, peeled and
  sliced
1 pound ripe tomatoes, peeled and
  seeded (or 1 cup canned)
1 teaspoon Hungarian sweet
  paprika
Salt and pepper to taste

Melt the butter in a skillet and sauté the onions until they are golden brown. Add the green peppers; stir and cook for 2 minutes. Add the potatoes, mixing well with the onion and green pepper. Cover the skillet, lower the heat, and cook for 15 to 20 minutes or until the potatoes are soft. Do not allow the potatoes to scorch. Uncover, add the tomatoes and seasonings, and cook for another 10 minutes.

The Crispiest Potatoes for a Crowd

½ cup melted butter, preferably
  clarified
5 pounds all-purpose potatoes

Preheat the oven to 450 degrees. Brush the bottom of a 17-inch jelly-roll pan with the melted butter.

Peel the potatoes and keep them covered with water.

Cut a thin slice from the long side of a potato, place it, cut side down, on a board and cut it into ⅛-inch slices. Holding the potato with all slices together place it in the jelly-roll pan, separating the slices to lie in an overlapping row. Continue until you have 4 or 5 long lines of sliced potatoes, filling the pan. Pour the butter over all the surfaces and bake for 30 minutes. Lower the temperature to 375 degrees and bake for about 30 minutes more, depending on your preference for softness or crispness.

Pass the salt and pepper at the table.

Sweet Potatoes

Sweet potatoes are an American treat—easy to cook and delicious, skin and all. Thanksgiving dinner menus traditionally couple sweet potatoes with turkey. Bake them while the turkey is roasting, or prepare a Sweet Potato Pie, which can be made ahead of time.

Sweet Potato Pie

Serves 6-8

3 pounds sweet potatoes
½ pound unsalted butter
4 tablespoons brown sugar or maple syrup
10-ounce can crushed pineapple or 1 cup applesauce

Preheat the oven to 350 degrees.

Scrub the potatoes and cook them in boiling water to cover until they are soft, about 15 minutes. Cool and peel the potatoes, then mash them. Add 4 tablespoons butter, 2 tablespoons sugar or maple syrup and the desired fruit. Spoon the mixture into a 10-inch round ovenproof dish, dot it with the remaining butter, and sprinkle the top with the remaining sugar. * Bake for 35 to 45 minutes or until it is crusty.

NOTE: For children, place a few marshmallows on top of the pie just before removing it from the oven.

Additions of lemon or orange juice, brandy or rum are tasty variations.

Pumpkin

Autumn has to be the most magnificent season in the Northeast. The farms are laden with pumpkins and odd-shaped squash in vibrant colors, an inspiration to any artist. Yet many people who like to look at pumpkins never think of cooking them. Treat the pumpkin like any winter squash or even like a potato.

Pumpkin is a beautiful vegetable for presentation. You may use it, for instance, as a natural tureen for soup or stew. Wash the pumpkin and cut across the top to form a lid. Use the stalk on top as a handle. Clean out the cavity, fill it with hot soup or stew, and heat it in the oven at 350 degrees for 15 minutes.

Mashed Pumpkin

Serves 6

2- to 3-pound pumpkin
1 pound potatoes
2 tablespoons butter
½ pound onions, chopped
¼ cup heavy cream
2 ounces Monterey Jack cheese, diced
Salt and pepper to taste
1 tablespoon finely chopped parsley or fresh chervil, if available

Wash and peel the pumpkin and the potatoes. Remove the seeds and fibrous strings from the cavity of the pumpkin and cut the meat into large chunks. Cut the potatoes into chunks too, and cook them with the pumpkin in a saucepan with salted water to cover until they are tender, about 25 minutes.

Melt the butter in a skillet and sauté the chopped onions until they are glazed. Add the heavy cream and cheese; remove from the heat.

When the pumpkin and the potato feel soft to the touch of a fork, pour off the liquid and mash the vegetables. Add the cream mixture and season it with salt and pepper. * Heat it until it is piping hot, stirring constantly. Garnish it with parsley or chervil and serve immediately.

NOTE: This may be prepared several hours or a day or two ahead. Place the pumpkin in an ovenproof dish; bake in the oven at 350 degrees for 10 to 15 minutes or until it is hot.

Spinach

Spinach requires more patience and time to clean than to cook. Tear off and discard the roots and stems. Fill a basin or sink with cold water. Swirl the spinach in the water to release the sand and let it soak for 5 minutes. Gently remove the spinach to a colander so as not to disturb sand that has settled to the bottom, then repeat the process. Two rinsings should be adequate.

The two recipes that follow are the simplest methods of cooking spinach; I have used the first for as long as I can remember, and the second since the advent of the processor. One of my favorite meals is a very simple one—young spinach, a baked potato, and a lamb chop.

Steamed Spinach
Serves 3-4

1 pound spinach, washed
Salt, pepper and nutmeg to taste
Butter and/or cream

Stuff wet spinach into a 2- or 3-quart saucepan to fit snugly. Cover and turn the heat on high; when the cover is hot, turn the heat down. Cook for 3 or 4 minutes. Season to taste. Toss with butter or cream as desired.

Processor Spinach
Serves 3-4

1 tablespoon butter
2 shallots
1 pound spinach, washed
¼ teaspoon nutmeg
Salt and pepper to taste
2 tablespoons heavy cream

As you melt the butter in a skillet, mince the shallots in the processor. Add the shallots to the skillet and cook just enough to glaze them. Puree the spinach in the processor (in 2 batches, if necessary). Add it to the skillet and stir in the seasonings and cream. * Cook on high heat for a few minutes, then serve immediately.

Spinach Casserole

This is a quickly prepared and popular dish; three very hungry people have been known to finish it off in one sitting.

2 pounds spinach or 2 10-ounce
   packages frozen chopped spinach
¼ pound cream cheese at room
   temperature
Salt and pepper to taste
2 tablespoons butter

Preheat the oven to 350 degrees.

Wash the spinach well and stuff it into a 3- or 4-quart covered saucepan with only the water that clings to the leaves. Bring it to a boil, uncover, and cook it for 2 to 3 minutes or until it is tender to your taste. Press out the excess water through a strainer.

Puree the spinach in a processor or chop it coarsely by hand. Blend it well with the cream cheese and season it to taste; then turn it into a 1-quart casserole or an 8-inch shallow baking dish. Dot it with butter and bake for 15 minutes, until it is piping hot.

Steamed Spinach Salad

Here it is! A theatrical spinach and mushroom salad made famous by an anonymous actor-chef. With the proper backdrop you can provide the drama and the lunch.

1 pound fresh spinach
¼ pound mushrooms
1 tablespoon olive oil
2 cloves garlic, peeled and
   left whole
6 strips lean bacon, diced
¼ cup wine vinegar
Salt and pepper to taste

Use a 10- or 12-inch round china or wooden salad bowl.

Wash the spinach following the directions given previously. Dry it in a spinner or in a dishcloth. Tear it into bite-sized pieces and arrange it in the salad bowl.

Wipe the mushrooms; slice them thinly and toss them over the salad. Cover all with absorbent paper and refrigerate it until ready to use. This may be done several hours ahead.

When ready to serve, bring the salad bowl near the stove. Heat the oil in a 12-inch skillet or one that will cover the salad bowl. Sauté the garlic for a few minutes, taking care not to let it burn. Discard the garlic; add the bacon and fry until it is crisp. Add the vinegar to the skillet. Immediately invert the pan over the salad bowl and hold it there for 1 minute, steaming the spinach slightly. Uncover; add salt and pepper to taste. Toss the salad well and serve.

Spinach Dumplings (Gnocchi Verdi)

The spinach mixture which fills these Italian dumplings also makes a perfect filling for crêpes.

1½ pounds spinach
4 scallions
1½ cups ricotta cheese
1 cup breadcrumbs
2 eggs, beaten
½ cup grated Parmesan cheese
1 teaspoon basil
½ teaspoon freshly grated nutmeg
Salt and pepper to taste
1 cup flour
¼ cup heavy cream

Wash the spinach well and dry it thoroughly. Chop the scallions and the spinach finely in a processor and transfer them to a mixing bowl. Add the ricotta, breadcrumbs, eggs, ¼ cup Parmesan cheese, basil and nutmeg and beat them with a wooden spoon or in an electric mixer. Season with salt and pepper to taste. Refrigerate for at least 2 hours.

Spread the flour on a sheet of wax paper. Take a heaping tablespoon of the spinach mixture and roll it into a 3-inch sausage shape with your hands, then roll it in the flour. Continue in this manner until all of the mixture is used. Pour ¼ cup of cream into a 9-by-13-inch baking dish.

Boil at least 2 inches of salted water in a deep skillet. Reduce to a simmer and immerse 6 to 8 dumplings at a time. The dumplings are cooked when they float to the top. Remove them with a slotted spoon, draining off all the water. Place them neatly in a line in the baking dish, and repeat until all the dumplings are cooked. Distribute the remaining Parmesan cheese over all the dumplings. * Bake for 10 minutes.

NOTE: The spinach mixture can also be spooned into a casserole, topped with ½ cup heavy cream and ¼ cup Parmesan cheese, and baked at 375 degrees for 30 minutes.

Spinach Rolls

This recipe, adapted from Escoffier, can be served as an appetizer or for a light lunch.

4 tablespoons butter
1 pound fresh spinach
2¾ teaspoons salt
1 shallot, diced
2 slices white bread, crusts removed
3 tablespoons flour
1 cup milk or chicken broth
¼ teaspoon pepper
¼ teaspoon nutmeg (optional)
¼ cup grated Gruyère cheese
¼ cup grated Parmesan cheese

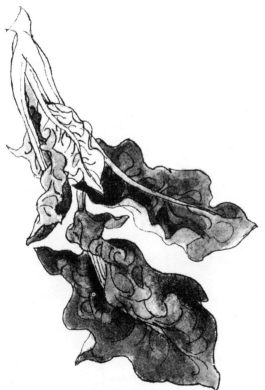

Preheat the oven to 350 degrees and grease a baking sheet with 2 tablespoons of the butter.

Wash the spinach and remove the tough stems. Choose 24 of the largest leaves and set them aside. Set out a bowl of cold water and paper towels for blotting.

Boil 2 quarts of water with 2 teaspoons of salt. Immerse 3 leaves at a time into the water to blanch them. Boil them for 15 seconds, remove them with a slotted spoon, and cool them immediately in cold water. Spread each leaf out carefully, one on top of the other, on the paper towels. When you have finished, you will have 8 sets of 3 leaves each. Press the paper towels on them to dry them.

Blanch the remaining spinach in boiling water for 1 minute. Drain and puree it in the blender with the shallot.

Cut the bread into tiny cubes. Toast the cubes on a greased baking sheet in the oven until they are light brown.

Heat the remaining 2 tablespoons of butter in a heavy saucepan. Stir in the flour and add the milk or broth gradually. Add the seasonings and 1 tablespoon each of the cheeses. When the sauce has thickened, add ¼ cup of sauce to the puree of spinach. Mix in the toasted bread cubes and adjust the seasoning to taste.

Place a spoonful of the puree mixture on each set of spinach leaves, roll the leaves over and fold them like an envelope. Place the rolls in the buttered baking dish, top them with the remaining sauce and scatter the remaining cheese over the surface. Bake, uncovered, for 15 minutes.

Squash

There are many interesting varieties of squash that offer the cook numerous options. Summer squash may be white, yellow or green (zucchini); it is harvested young and all varieties have thin skins. Winter squash is hard-shelled; the best-known varieties are acorn, butternut, hubbard, turban and buttercup. Pumpkins are in this gourd category too.

Recipes for summer squash can be used with all varieties. Similarly, the recipes for several kinds of winter squash are interchangeable.

Baked Acorn Squash

Serves 4

2 medium acorn squash (3 pounds)
4 teaspoons butter
4 tablespoons dark brown sugar

Preheat the oven to 375 degrees. Fill a 9-by-13-inch oven-proof dish with 1 inch of hot water.

Cut the squash in half and scoop out the seeds. Place 1 teaspoon of butter and 1 tablespoon of brown sugar in the cavity of each half squash. Place the squash in the baking pan and bake it for 45 minutes to 1 hour, depending on the size of the squash.

NOTE: An attractive and delicious variation is to fill each cavity with a mixture of ½ cup fresh cranberries and 3 tablespoons sugar. Insert 2 slices of orange into the cranberries and bake as described above.

Chunky Butternut Squash

Serves 4

1 butternut squash (2 pounds)
1 teaspoon salt
2 tablespoons butter
¼ cup maple syrup

Peel the squash as you would a potato. Cut it in half vertically, remove the seeds, and cut it into chunks.

Cook the squash for 15 minutes in salted water to barely cover it. Drain, and add the butter and maple syrup. Simmer until the liquid has been absorbed into the squash.

NOTE: I like to prepare this recipe in large quantities and freeze extra portions for use later in the winter.

Baked Summer Squash

8-10 small squash (about 2 pounds)
½ cup finely chopped shallots
3 tablespoons olive oil or butter
½ cup breadcrumbs
Salt and pepper to taste

Preheat the oven to 350 degrees and grease a 9-by-13-inch ovenproof dish with 1 tablespoon oil or butter.

Scrub the squash. Bring 3 quarts of salted water to a boil and cook the squash for 2 minutes, until they are barely soft. Immediately immerse them in ice-cold water. Drain and dry them.

Sauté the shallots in olive oil or butter until they are glazed. Remove them from the heat to a bowl and add the breadcrumbs, and salt and pepper to taste.

Sprinkle half the shallot mixture evenly on the bottom of the baking dish. Slice the squash in half lengthwise. Score each cut side 3 times (⅛ inch deep). Place a layer of halves in the dish; the halves may be crisscrossed for a second layer if necessary. Sprinkle the remaining shallot mixture on top. Bake, covered, for 20 minutes. Uncover and bake 10 minutes, until lightly browned.

Barbecued Stuffed Zucchini

This recipe is perfect for outdoor cooking.

4 medium-size zucchini (1½ pounds)
1 onion, finely chopped
2 tablespoons butter, softened
¼ cup breadcrumbs
1 teaspoon salt
¼ teaspoon pepper
1 teaspoon chervil
1 tablespoon finely chopped parsley

Cut off one lengthwise slice from each zucchini about ¼ inch thick, and discard it. Scoop out the squash without tearing the skin, chop the scooped-out portion very finely, and blend it with all the other ingredients. Stuff the zucchini shells, wrap each piece in heavy aluminum foil, and broil for 30 minutes on an outdoor grill, turning occasionally.

NOTE: To prepare indoors, preheat the oven to 375 degrees. Do not wrap the squash in foil; bake in a covered casserole for 35 to 40 minutes. Uncover the casserole for the final 5 minutes to allow the zucchini to brown.

Quick Zucchini

4 medium-size zucchini (1½ pounds)
1 tablespoon butter or oil
1 small onion, diced
1 clove garlic or 2 slices ginger root
   (optional)
¼ cup water or broth
Salt and pepper to taste
1 tablespoon finely chopped parsley

Scrub the zucchini well; certain varieties are sandy. To peel or not to peel is a matter of personal preference; young garden varieties do not need it. Peel it very thinly if you have to, leaving some green color. Grate the zucchini using a processor or the coarse side of a hand grater.

Heat the butter in a skillet; add the onion and garlic. (Use oil if your choice is ginger root.) Cook until the onion is glazed. Add the zucchini and stir, pour in the water, and cook, covered, for 1 minute. Uncover and cook for another 1 to 2 minutes. Season to taste and garnish with parsley.

Spaghetti Squash

This squash makes an unusual first course—a vegetable pasta.

1 spaghetti squash (2-3 pounds)
1 cup heavy cream
1 bouquet garni (bay leaf, thyme
    and parsley tied together in a
    cheesecloth bag)
2 ounces ham, diced
2 ounces Gruyère cheese, grated
Pinch cayenne
Salt and pepper to taste
1 tablespoon finely chopped parsley

Put the squash in a saucepan with salted water to cover it by at least ½ inch. Cover the saucepan and boil the squash for 30 minutes, or until the outer skin feels slightly soft to the touch.

While the squash is cooking, simmer the cream with the bouquet garni for 5 minutes. It will reduce to about ¾ cup. Discard the bouquet garni.

Remove the squash to a cutting board. Split it in half vertically and remove the seeds and fibrous strings. Place it on an oval platter.

Stir the ham, cheese and seasonings into the cream and place over high heat for 3 minutes. Pour the cream mixture into the cavities of the squash and garnish with the chopped parsley.

Bring the squash to the table and, with dramatic gestures, use a large fork and spoon to pull strands of squash out of the shell—it *does* look like spaghetti.

Tomatoes

Raw or cooked, the tomato is one of our most popular and versatile fruit-vegetables. Commercial growers have cultivated a very hardy variety that suffers from a thick skin and less flavor than home-grown tomatoes, but in the summer and early fall, even these commercially grown tomatoes can be delicious.

Tomato Slices with Cheese
Serves 4

1 tablespoon butter
4 medium-size tomatoes
2 ounces Roquefort, blue cheese or
    goat cheese
3 ounces cream cheese
2 tablespoons milk or cream
¼ teaspoon white pepper
Dash cayenne
16 sesame crackers
8 anchovies (optional)

Preheat the oven to 375 degrees and butter an 11-by-15-inch jelly-roll pan.

Cut each tomato into about 4 slices at least ¼ inch thick. Blend the Roquefort, cream cheese and milk into a smooth paste. Season it with the pepper and cayenne, and spread each slice of tomato lightly with the cheese mixture. Place the tomatoes in a pan and bake them for 10 minutes or put them under the broiler for 2 minutes. Place each tomato slice on a sesame cracker and serve. If desired, garnish the top with half an anchovy.

NOTE: Try filling scooped-out cherry tomatoes with the same cheese mixture. Pop them under the broiler for 1 minute.

Creamy Green Tomatoes
Serves 4-6

6 large green tomatoes
½ cup flour
¼ pound butter
¼ cup brown sugar
1 teaspoon salt
¼ teaspoon pepper
2 tablespoons sherry vinegar
1 cup heavy cream

Cut each tomato into 3 thick slices and dredge them in the flour. Melt the butter in a large skillet and fry the tomatoes quickly on one side. Sprinkle about ½ teaspoon brown sugar on each slice and turn it over. Sprinkle the tomatoes with the salt, pepper, vinegar and the remaining brown sugar. The sugar will caramelize as the tomatoes brown. Pour in the cream and cook until the cream is hot. Serve immediately.

NOTE: Omit the cream if you are counting calories.

Low-Calorie Stuffed Tomatoes

Serves 4

4 fresh ripe tomatoes (1½ pounds)
1 onion, diced
2 ribs of celery, diced
½ pound mushrooms, diced
1 clove garlic, finely chopped
Salt and pepper to taste
½ teaspoon chili pepper
1 teaspoon basil
2 tablespoons orange juice

Preheat the oven to 375 degrees.

Cut across each tomato at the stem end. Scoop out the pulp and reserve it.

Heat a skillet. Brown the onion in the dry, hot skillet, stirring as needed to keep the onion from scorching. Add the celery, mushrooms and garlic. Cover the skillet, lower the heat, and cook for 2 or 3 minutes. Add the tomato pulp and the remaining ingredients.

Fill the tomato shells with this mixture and bake, uncovered, for 10 minutes in an 8-inch ovenproof dish.

Turnips

Turnips are often considered lowly vegetables, but they are a staple in my refrigerator; they are zesty in soups and stews and store just as well as carrots.

The rutabaga is a turnip of a different color and season. This large yellow root can be cooked like a potato, mashed and buttered, or combined with carrots and potatoes.

Glazed Turnips

Serves 4

It is important to buy turnips of uniform size for presentation. Many people will not recognize them in a lovely brown glaze.

4 medium-size white turnips
3 tablespoons clarified butter
Pinch sugar
Salt and pepper to taste

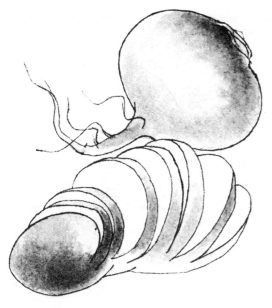

Grease a 12-inch skillet with 1 tablespoon butter.

Wash and peel the turnips. Cover them with salted water and bring them to a boil in a covered saucepan. Cook them for 8 to 10 minutes, until they are just tender but not soft. Remove the turnips to a board and let them cool slightly, until you can handle them easily. Cut each one into 5 or 6 slices, keeping each turnip intact.

Place each turnip, fanned out slightly to show the slices, in the skillet with 1 tablespoon butter. Keep each turnip apart from the others.*

Heat the skillet until the butter melts and starts sizzling. Add more butter to the pan as the turnips brown slightly. Turn each turnip over carefully with a spatula to keep its slices together as a unit. Add the remaining butter and the pinch of sugar to the pan. Heating and glazing the turnips will take no more than 3 or 4 minutes. Serve them immediately, 1 turnip per person.

Casseroles, Tarts and Combinations

This title speaks for itself. Some of these vegetable combinations are traditional recipes, some are my own creations and some have been gleaned from friends. They should inspire many new ideas in your own kitchen.

Four-Vegetable Tart

Serves 6-8

2-pound eggplant
1½ pounds zucchini
½ teaspoon salt
¼ cup flour
1½ cups vegetable oil
1 tablespoon butter
1 teaspoon finely chopped garlic
2 tablespoons finely chopped parsley
⅛ teaspoon thyme
⅛ teaspoon marjoram
Black pepper to taste
2 tablespoons breadcrumbs
½ cup Duxelles (recipe on page 51)
8-12 cherry tomatoes

Preheat the oven to 400 degrees and set out a 9-inch quiche pan or a shallow 9-inch round ovenproof dish. Do not grease.

Cut off and discard the stem end of the eggplant. Slice the eggplant lengthwise into pieces, about ⅛ inch thick.

Peel and grate the zucchini and put it in a colander. Sprinkle with ½ teaspoon salt, toss to combine, and set the colander over a container to allow the liquid to drain. (The zucchini need not be peeled if it is very fresh and young.)

Dredge the eggplant slices in the flour, shaking off the excess. Heat the oil to 350 degrees in a deep skillet and set out paper towels for blotting. Fry the eggplant, 2 or 3 pieces at a time, until the slices are evenly browned. Drain on the paper towels. (An alternate method is to broil the eggplant sprinkled lightly with oil.)

Heat the butter in a skillet and sauté the garlic for 1 min-

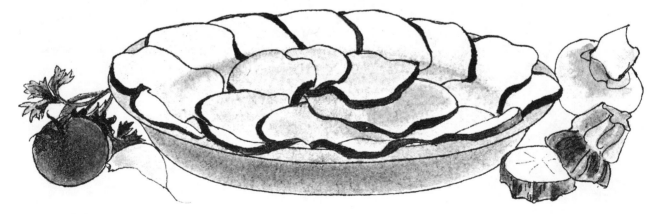

ute without browning it. Press the zucchini against the colander to discard as much juice as possible. Add the zucchini to the skillet; stir and cook it for 3 to 4 minutes. Stir in the parsley, thyme and marjoram and season with black pepper to taste. Remove from the heat.

Lay the slices of eggplant, overlapping slightly, on the bottom of the baking dish, bringing the wide end of each slice up along the rim of the pan. Use only 1 layer of the eggplant to cover the bottom and sides of the pan, as if you were forming a tart shell. Sprinkle the breadcrumbs on the eggplant.

Spread the duxelles evenly over the eggplant slices, then spread the zucchini over the duxelles evenly to the sides, smoothing the top. Cut the cherry tomatoes in half and place them, cut side up, in a circle on the surface of the tart.*

Bake 15 minutes. If the baking pan has a removable bottom, let it cool for a few minutes and then remove the tart from the pan to a round platter. Garnish the center with a tomato rose (cut from tomato skins).

VARIATIONS:

1) Beat together 1 egg and ½ cup cream. Season with ¼ teaspoon salt and a dash of pepper and pour the mixture over the top of the tart before baking it.

2) Sprinkle ¼ cup each grated Gruyère and grated Parmesan cheese over the top before baking the tart.

3) Lay thin slices of mozzarella or fontina cheese on top before baking.

Julienne of Vegetables
Serves 2

I enjoy cutting the julienne strips by hand for just the two of us, but the processor comes in handy for larger numbers of guests.

1 large onion, peeled and slivered
2 ribs celery, cut in julienne
2 carrots, cut in julienne
1 turnip, cut in julienne
½ cup chicken broth
Salt and pepper to taste
1 tablespoon sherry vinegar
1 teaspoon savory

Combine the onion, celery, carrots and turnip in a saucepan with ¼ cup water. Cover and cook for 2 minutes. Uncover and add ¼ cup broth. Allow the liquid to evaporate, then repeat with the remainder of the broth. Season to taste; add the sherry vinegar and the savory.

NOTE: Added to 1 quart of clear broth, this recipe makes a delicious soup.

Herbed Vegetables in a Pot

Serves 4-6

This home-style vegetable potpourri makes a hearty fall meal. The amounts can be varied to suit your taste and vegetable supply. Use broth instead of cream if you are counting calories.

2 tablespoons butter or oil
2 onions, thinly sliced
2 potatoes, thinly sliced
2 tablespoons mixed chervil, thyme
   and parsley
Salt and pepper to taste
1 carrot, sliced
¼ cup water or chicken broth
6 mushrooms, sliced
2 yellow or green squash, sliced
   in rounds
½ cup heavy cream or chicken broth

Heat the butter or oil in a 2-quart saucepan. Cook the onions until they are just golden and wilted. Add the potatoes and cook on high heat so that they brown slightly with the onions.

Sprinkle a small amount of the mixed herbs, salt and pepper on the potatoes. Add a layer of the carrots and pour on the water or broth. Cover and cook for 7 to 8 minutes, until the potatoes are almost tender. Add more herbs, salt and pepper.

Next arrange a layer of the mushrooms, plus the herbs and seasonings, and a layer of squash, again adding herbs and seasoning.

Pour the cream or broth over all, being careful not to disturb the layers.

Cover it and simmer for 5 minutes.

Onion Tart

Serves 6

Tarte à l'oignon is an Alsatian specialty. For a tangy, authentic touch, substitute sour cream.

1 unbaked 8-inch pie shell
1 tablespoon Dijon mustard
1 tablespoon butter
1½ pounds onions, peeled and thinly
   sliced
1 egg yolk
2 eggs
¾ cup light or heavy cream
¾ teaspoon salt
¼ teaspoon pepper
Pinch cayenne

Preheat the oven to 400 degrees.

Spread the mustard evenly over the pie shell. Pierce the bottom several times with a fork so that it does not bubble. Bake it for 5 minutes, then remove to a rack to cool.

Heat the butter in a skillet. Sauté the onions until they are glazed and wilted but not browned. Cool them slightly and then spread them evenly over the pastry shell.

Beat the egg yolk and eggs, add the light cream and the seasonings, and pour the mixture over the onions. Place the pie on the middle rack of the oven and bake it for 30 minutes, or until it is set.

NOTE: Ham or rendered bacon on the bottom of the pie shell will make a tasty addition.

Wheat Berry Pilaf

Wheat berries are whole dried seeds of wheat from which we get cracked wheat (bulgur) and flour. This grain can be handled like dried beans and cooked like brown rice. Wheat berries are nutritious, crunchy and delicious, and may be purchased at health food or specialty food stores.

To prepare wheat berries for cooking, either soak them overnight in water to cover, or bring them to a boil in water to cover, simmer for 3 minutes, turn off the heat and leave them covered for 1 hour. Then drain them.

3 tablespoons butter
½ cup diced onions
½ cup diced mushrooms
1 cup wheat berries
2 cups chicken broth or water
2 tablespoons rice
2 tablespoons bulgur (cracked wheat)
Salt and pepper to taste

Preheat the oven to 350 degrees and grease a 2-quart casserole with 1 tablespoon of the butter.

Heat 2 tablespoons butter in a small skillet, add the onions and mushrooms, and cook them until the onions are wilted but not browned.

Combine the wheat berries, the onion mixture and the broth in a 3-quart saucepan, bring to a boil, reduce the heat, and simmer until the berries are soft, 40 to 50 minutes. Add the rice and bulgur 12 minutes before the wheat berries are done.

Spoon the mixture into the prepared casserole and bake it for 10 minutes, stirring occasionally to prevent the top from drying too much.

NOTE: The cooking time for wheat berries will depend greatly upon how long they have been stored. If they were freshly dried, cooking time will be shorter.

Eggplant Florentine

3 tablespoons butter
2-pound eggplant (or 2 smaller
 ones)
2 cloves garlic, finely chopped
2 onions, diced
1 pound ground beef, veal, lamb
 or pork
2 tablespoons flour
2 tablespoons breadcrumbs
1 cup chopped tomatoes
Salt and pepper to taste
½ teaspoon basil
½ pound mozzarella cheese, cut
 in strips
1 pound spinach, cooked (recipes on
 page 61)

Preheat the oven to 350 degrees and grease a 15-inch oval ovenproof dish with 1 tablespoon of the butter.

Cut the eggplant in half lengthwise. Scoop out the inside, leaving a ½-inch-thick shell. Cube the scooped-out portion of the eggplant.

Heat the remaining butter in a heavy skillet. Add the garlic and onions and sauté them until they are golden brown. Add the ground meat, separating the pieces of meat with a fork while browning them.

Roll the eggplant cubes in a mixture of the flour and breadcrumbs, then stir them into the meat mixture, and brown for 2 to 3 minutes. Remove from the heat.

Stir in the tomatoes, salt, pepper and basil. Taste it and adjust the seasoning. Fill the eggplant skins, set them in the baking dish, and bake for 1 hour.

Place the cheese strips over the eggplant 5 minutes before serving and put the baking dish under the broiler for 30 seconds. Spoon the hot spinach around the stuffed eggplant halves and serve as a main course.

Cauliflower Tart

1 tablespoon butter
½ cup breadcrumbs
2 tablespoons flour
½ cup grated cheddar, Gruyère, or
 Parmesan cheese
1 medium-size head cauliflower,
 cooked in florets
1 cup sour cream
2 eggs
Salt and white pepper to taste

Preheat the oven to 375 degrees and butter a 9-inch pie plate or ovenproof dish.

Stir together the breadcrumbs, flour and cheese. Pat half of this mixture into the pie plate. Arrange the cooked cauliflower in an even layer on top.

Stir together the sour cream, eggs, salt and pepper, pour the mixture over the cauliflower, and sprinkle the remainder of the crumb mixture on the top. * Bake for 20 minutes.

NOTE: This dish can be prepared 2 hours ahead and baked just before serving.

Flan of Carrots and Parsnips

½ pound carrots, peeled and sliced
½ pound parsnips, peeled and sliced
1½ teaspoons salt
2 tablespoons butter
2 eggs
½ cup light cream
½ teaspoon white pepper
1 tablespoon freshly chopped chives

Preheat the oven to 375 degrees. Use a pan large enough to hold 6 4-ounce custard cups; pour in 1 inch of hot water and set the pan on the middle rack of the oven.

Boil the carrots and parsnips in salted water to cover for 10 to 15 minutes, or until they are soft. Drain off the water.

Puree the carrots and parsnips in a food processor. Add the butter; scrape down the bowl. Add the eggs, light cream and the salt and pepper. Taste, and adjust the seasoning.

Spoon the mixture into the custard cups and place these in the simmering water. Bake for 35 minutes, then remove and let them rest for 5 minutes. Gently loosen each mold by inserting a knife around the edge. Shake the dish and unmold.

Garnish the tops with chives or sprigs of parsley.

Purees

Purees are smooth mixtures of one or more cooked vegetables that are easily prepared in a blender or food processor. Simple to cook and reheat, purees may also be used as vegetable bases for sauces and, when thinned with broth, make excellent soups.

Root and starchy vegetables have enough body of their own and need only be cooked with water and seasoning; watery vegetables should be combined with a small amount of potato, rice, béchamel sauce or cream.

To be sure that a puree remains soft and creamy and does not form a crust, place a buttered round of wax paper on top of the mixture and heat it in the top part of a double boiler before serving it.

Green Bean Puree   *Serves 6*

Green bean puree is a delicious accompaniment to a roast. To achieve body, mashed cooked potato or a flour-based sauce must be added.

1 pound green beans
2 tablespoons butter
1 onion, finely chopped
½ cup Velouté Sauce (recipe on
   page 81)
½ teaspoon savory
Salt and pepper

Wash the beans, snap off the ends, and cut them into 1-inch slices. Bring 3 quarts of salted water to a boil, immerse the beans, and cook, covered, just until the water boils again. Uncover and cook until the green beans are soft, about 5 minutes. (They should be softer for puree than when eaten whole.) Drain off the water and set the beans aside.

Melt the butter in a skillet; when the foam subsides, add the onion and cook it until it is glazed. Place the beans, sautéed onion, velouté sauce and savory in a processor and blend for 1 minute. Pour the mixture into a bowl and adjust the seasoning with salt and pepper. Cover the surface with buttered wax paper. * Heat over simmering water in a double boiler.

NOTE: The puree can be prepared up to a day in advance and refrigerated.

Puree of Four Vegetables

Having root vegetables in my pantry as "standbys" when there was little time for marketing inspired this useful recipe.

1 small celery root (or 1 heart of celery)
1 medium-size potato
1 large carrot
1 medium parsnip or turnip
½ teaspoon salt
2 tablespoons cream (optional)
Salt and pepper to taste

Peel and slice the vegetables, then place them in a saucepan with salted water just to cover. Cover the saucepan and boil for about 7 minutes or until the vegetables are soft. Drain off the water (reserving it for broth and stews) and puree the vegetables in a processor, food mill or blender. Add the cream; taste it and adjust the seasonings.

Remove it to a bowl; cover the top of the puree with a buttered round of wax paper. * Heat over boiling water in the top part of a double boiler.

Puree of Peas

2 tablespoons butter
2 tablespoons finely chopped shallots
1 cup chicken broth
4 pounds fresh peas or 2 10-ounce boxes frozen peas
Salt and pepper to taste
2 tablespoons cream
⅛ teaspoon nutmeg
⅛ teaspoon curry powder

Heat the butter in a saucepan until it sizzles, but do not let it brown. Add the shallots and cook them for 2 minutes. Pour in the chicken broth and bring it to a boil. Add the peas and cook, covered, for 8 minutes or, if frozen, according to the directions on the box. Do not overcook them. Take the cover off toward the end of the cooking time so that the peas stay green and the liquid almost evaporates. Puree the peas in a food processor. Add the salt and pepper, cream, nutmeg and curry powder.

Leek Puree

Leeks tend to be scarce and therefore rather expensive in many parts of the United States. If they are readily available, though, a leek puree is an unusual and delicious side dish. (You might consider buying leeks in large quantities and freezing them; leek soup in winter is quite a treat. Wash and dry the leeks well, without cutting them, and freeze.)

2 pounds leeks
1 cup chicken broth
4 tablespoons butter
Salt and pepper

Trim the root ends and cut off the dark green leaves. Split the roots of the leeks vertically and wash them very well as they will probably be sandy. Cut into 1-inch slices.

Place the leeks in a saucepan with ¼ cup broth and 2 tablespoons butter. Simmer, stirring constantly, for 4 to 5 minutes; do not let them brown. Add the remainder of the broth, cover, and simmer for at least 35 to 40 minutes. The leeks must be very limp. Add more broth if necessary.

When the leeks are extremely soft, puree them in a processor, food mill or blender. Add the butter and seasonings. Remove to a bowl covered with a round of buttered wax paper. * Heat over boiling water in a double boiler.

Tomato Puree

2 pounds fresh, ripe tomatoes
2 tablespoons butter
¼ cup chopped shallots
1 medium-size onion, chopped
Salt and pepper to taste
1 bay leaf
1 sprig Italian parsley
Pinch sugar

Skin the tomatoes by plunging them into boiling water to cover for 30 seconds, then into cold water. Cut the peeled tomatoes in half horizontally. Squeeze out the seeds and juices and puree the tomatoes in a blender or food processor.

Heat the butter in a 2-quart saucepan. Add the shallots and cook for a few minutes to wilt and glaze them. Add the tomato puree and the remaining ingredients. Simmer, uncovered, for 10 to 15 minutes until a thick puree is formed. Adjust the seasonings and serve hot.

NOTE: For an elegant and glossy appearance, the puree may be further prepared as follows:

Strain the puree through a sieve. It will seem watery; cook it again to reduce it or add 1 teaspoon arrowroot or cornstarch mixed with 1 tablespoon cold water to thicken it. This version makes an attractive backdrop on a plate for an individual vegetable mold or even 3 florets of cauliflower.

Hot Sauces

The following sauces are used with hot vegetables that have been either boiled or steamed.

Velouté Sauce

Makes 2 cups

4 tablespoons butter
6 tablespoons flour
2½ cups well-seasoned chicken
   broth or vegetable broth, heated
Salt and pepper to taste

Heat the butter. Add the flour and stir well to form a roux. Cook the roux for 2 minutes on very low heat, then remove it from the heat and add the warm broth gradually, stirring it well. Continue cooking over a low flame for 20 minutes, stirring occasionally, until the sauce is thick. Adjust the seasoning to taste.

Béchamel (White Sauce)

Makes 1¾ cups

4 tablespoons butter
5 tablespoons flour
2 cups milk or light cream, heated
1¼ teaspoons salt
½ teaspoon white pepper
Optional seasonings: dry mustard,
    cayenne, Tabasco or nutmeg

Heat the butter in a saucepan. Add the flour and stir over low heat for 2 minutes. Take the saucepan off the heat.

Gradually stir in ½ cup of the milk or cream. Pour in the remaining liquid and add the seasoning.

Return the saucepan to the heat and continue stirring with a wooden spoon or whisk until the mixture thickens and comes to a boil. Cook over very low heat for a few minutes, stirring constantly.

CHEESE SAUCE

Add 4 ounces of sharp grated cheese to the Béchamel Sauce.

DILL SAUCE

4 tablespoons chopped fresh dill
2 tablespoons chopped parsley
3 tablespoons lemon juice

Add the dill and parsley to the Béchamel Sauce. Cook over low flame for 5 minutes, then add the lemon juice.

Quick Hollandaise

Makes about 1 cup

½ pound butter
3 egg yolks
2 tablespoons lemon juice
½ teaspoon salt
Dash of cayenne

Heat the butter until it bubbles, but do not brown it.

Put the egg yolks, lemon juice and the seasonings into a blender or processor. Turn the machine on for a few seconds, then off. Turn it on again at low speed and add the butter very, very slowly into the egg yolks. The mixture will thicken. Stop the machine as soon as all the butter has been absorbed and the mixture has emulsified.

This sauce can be used immediately or kept warm over hot water in a double boiler.

Fresh Tomato Sauce

2 tablespoons oil or butter
2 onions, finely chopped
5 pounds ripe tomatoes, peeled,
   seeded and diced
2 teaspoons salt
½ teaspoon pepper
½ teaspoon sugar
2 tablespoons lemon juice
½ teaspoon dried basil (or 1 fresh
   leaf)

Heat the oil in a large heavy saucepan and add the onions. When the onions are glazed (but not browned), add all the other ingredients. Simmer, uncovered, stirring occasionally, until the mixture is reduced to a puree, about 1 hour.

NOTE: Wine or herbs may be added if desired, and the sauce may be strained.

Cold Sauces

The following sauces can be served with salads or with cooked or raw vegetables that are served cold or at room temperature.

Vinaigrette

1 teaspoon Dijon mustard
½ teaspoon salt
¼ teaspoon freshly ground pepper
2 tablespoons tarragon or wine
   vinegar
½ cup olive oil, or a combination of
   olive oil and oil of your choice

Stir together the mustard, salt, pepper and vinegar. Add the oil slowly and continue to stir vigorously. Taste and adjust the seasoning.

Creamy Dressing

1 small egg
½ teaspoon salt
¼ teaspoon pepper
1 teaspoon Dijon mustard
1 large shallot
1 small clove garlic (optional)
2 tablespoons tarragon or wine
   vinegar
1 tablespoon lemon juice
½ cup olive oil

Using a blender or processor, beat together the egg, salt, pepper, mustard, shallot, garlic, vinegar and lemon juice. Add the oil gradually, while continuing to beat. Taste and adjust the seasoning.

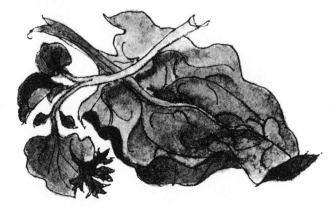

GREEN DRESSING

To a double recipe of Creamy Dressing, add ¼ cup each finely chopped parsley, spinach and watercress. If desired, moisture may be removed from the greens before chopping by blanching them in boiling water, plunging them in cold water and then squeezing out the moisture through cheesecloth.

Fresh Tomato Dressing

1 small onion, diced
1 tablespoon olive oil
1 pound fresh ripe tomatoes, peeled,
   seeded and chopped
Salt and pepper to taste
1 recipe Vinaigrette or Creamy
   Dressing (recipes on page 83)
1 tablespoon Cognac (optional)

Cook the onion in the olive oil. Add the tomatoes and cook over low heat for 15 minutes, or until soft. Strain through a sieve and season to taste with salt and pepper.

Add 2 tablespoons of this mixture to the dressing selected and add Cognac, if liked, for a distinctive touch.

NOTE: This dressing makes a very good base on which to serve slices of poached fish or chicken.